Effective RTI Training and Practices

Helping School and District Teams Improve Academic Performance and Social Behavior

Gary L. Cates
Craig Blum
Mark E. Swerdlik

Research Press
2612 North Mattis Avenue
Champaign, Illinois 61822
(800) 519-2707
www.researchpress.com

RESEARCH PRESS
PUBLISHERS

Copies of this book may be ordered from Research Press at the address given on the title page.

Composition by Jeff Helgesen
Cover design by Linda Brown, Positive I.D. Graphic Design, Inc.
Printed by Seaway Printing Co., Inc.

ISBN: 978–0-87822-648-1
Library of Congress Control Number 2010942801

To the hard-working and committed school personnel and their students who have taught us so much about RTI implementation

and

To our wives—Patricia Cates, Nancy Blum, and Peggy Swerdlik—who have supported us throughout the writing of this book; and to our children—Gary, William, Ryan, Andy, Jenny, and Danny—who have taught us so much about learning and development

Contents

Figures and Tables

Figures

Tables

Preface

We have consulted extensively with superintendents, principals, special education administrators, teachers, and support personnel such as school psychologists, social workers, reading specialists, and behavior interventionists on the implementation of Response to Intervention (RTI) for academic performance and social behavior domains. Throughout this process, we have come to realize that many schools in the United States face challenges in providing quality educational services to all students and eliminating achievement gaps between at-risk students and their peers. Moreover, we realize that these challenges often occur in a predictable sequence and at various stages of the RTI implementation process. Understanding this predictable sequence facilitates our effectiveness as consultants in that it not only allows us to help school personnel identify where they are developmentally in the RTI implementation process as a school, but also help them anticipate and prepare for both the immediate and distant challenges to come.

Based on our current understanding and accumulated experience, we wrote this book to provide school personnel with a general framework to deliver quality education and promote positive outcomes for all students. To accomplish this goal, we focus on training and implementation of RTI from a data-based decision-making perspective for both the academic performance and social behavior domains.

From a training standpoint, it is critical to have all school administrators and personnel informed to the greatest extent possible. Accompanying this book is a CD that contains PowerPoint slide shows based on Chapters 1–6. These slide shows are intended to assist personnel leading the RTI implementation and/or training by saving them the time of constructing their own presentations from scratch (the PowerPoint files can easily be modified or adapted based on the needs of the school or district).

From an implementation standpoint, it is critical to have the entire infrastructure in place in a systematic fashion in order maximize the positive outcomes of RTI. Toward that end, the CD also contains forms and templates to facilitate the implementation process.

Also, throughout the book, we provide specific examples based on our consulting experiences with schools. These examples help reinforce general concepts as well as your understanding of RTI procedures and processes.

We do not include a chapter that focuses specifically on data collection, analysis, and utilization. Instead, we infuse information about the various processes in all chapters, and we discuss current best practices for making data-based decisions related to universal screening, identifying students at risk, diagnostic testing, monitoring progress, evaluating intervention effectiveness, and evaluating systemwide RTI efforts. We do, however, include a chapter on effective problem solving and teaming to facilitate the data-based decision-making process.

We focus on academic performance and social behavior in all chapters because we recognize the importance of integrating both domains in an RTI model and emphasize that these two domains are not mutually exclusive. Because this integration of academic performance and social behavior represents a seemingly monumental task for trainers and school personnel who are implementing RTI, we provide a unified framework across both domains. As you read, you will find that the parallels between implementation of the academic performance and social behavior components of RTI are striking. By integrating this information and providing various supplemental resources, we hope to enable you to implement and facilitate the RTI process in a more seamless manner.

We wrote this book with the assumption that all children can learn, and our experience has taught us that effective RTI implementation can make the learning process more efficient and effective for all students.

Gary L. Cates
Craig Blum
Mark E. Swerdlik

November 26, 2010
Normal, IL

CHAPTER 1

Introduction to Response to Intervention

CHAPTER OVERVIEW

Based on our experiences in working with schools on implementing Response to Intervention (RTI) initiatives, we find that the efficiency and effectiveness of implementation are influenced by the extent to which key personnel have an understanding of the model. We cannot overstate the importance of this understanding. Moreover, it is important to correct the misinformation and resulting misunderstandings about RTI. The purpose of this chapter is to define and outline the principal components of RTI. More specifically, this chapter will:

- Provide a general understanding of RTI.
- Provide a rationale for RTI from both legal and scholarly perspectives.
- Present a model of a comprehensive tiered system of instructional support for academic performance and social behavior.
- Address how a continuum of assessment and instruction can be integrated within a tiered system of support.
- Provide an outline of a general comprehensive model of student support that also serves as a framework for the rest of this book.

UNDERSTANDING RESPONSE TO INTERVENTION

Definition: RTI Is About Meeting Educational Needs

Response to Intervention is a systems-based and preventive educational model that incorporates scientifically based measurement and instructional practices with systematic data collection, analysis, and decision making to meet the educational needs of all students in a school setting.

Perspective: RTI Is About Data-Based Decision Making

As evident in the definition, RTI relies heavily on data. Whether it be data collection, data entry, data analysis, and/or data-based decision-making rules, the topic of data is certainly a fundamental component of any effective RTI process. Therefore, the emphasis of this book is on data throughout the development, implementation, and evaluation of the RTI process.

Purpose: RTI Is About Evidence-Based Practices

The purposes of an RTI process of educational service delivery are to:

▫ Identify the educational needs of all students.

▫ Provide educational services to all students—and that match the needs of students.

▫ Prevent or minimize learning and social behavior problems.

▫ Foster an educational environment that implements instruction using highly effective and efficient educational practices to teach academics and social behavior.

Logic: RTI Is About Making Systematic Decisions

The logic of RTI is this: If a student is identified as needing support in order to meet minimal educational standards, we respond with an evidence-based support system to meet that need. Specifically, if a student is not successful given a well-implemented core or universal curriculum that we know is scientifically based and effective for the majority of students, we identify his or her potential learning or behavior problems early and attempt to address them in a systematic fashion. If a student responds to an intervention or instructional approach, we do not need to provide a more intensive level of the intervention or instruction.

RATIONALE FOR RESPONSE TO INTERVENTION

Legal Rationale: RTI Is About Accountability

No Child Left Behind Act

In January 2002, President George W. Bush signed the reauthorization of the Elementary and Secondary Education Act (ESEA), which is known as the No Child Left Behind Act of 2001 (NCLB). Among other goals, the No Child Left Behind Act addresses the "achievement gap" between groups such as the majority and students in historically low-achieving groups, including English language learners, members of various racial or ethnic groups, and students from low-income families. The act:

▫ Requires early intervention and accountability based on student outcomes.

▫ Requires states to utilize scientifically or evidence-based instruction.

▫ Requires states to develop challenging academic content standards for mathematics, reading or language arts, and science and create measurable achievement standards that all children are expected to meet.

▫ Requires states to conduct reliable and valid annual assessments of nationally recognized standards in each of the designated academic areas.

▫ Requires states to attain academic proficiency for all students by 2013 and begin documenting progress toward that goal. If schools do not meet achievement benchmarks, a series of increasingly negative sanctions are put into place. Minimal sanctions include requiring schools to provide supplemental tutoring. The most negative consequence imposed on the school is the state assuming control and the school staff being "reconstituted" (that is, most or all of the school's administration and staff are replaced or reassigned).

◻ Requires schools to report on their progress in meeting state achievement standards for various disaggregated groups. These groups include those of various racial or ethnic status (African Americans, Hispanics), English language learners, and students with disabilities.

The "high-stakes testing" movement that grew out of the mandates of NCLB and the schools' requirement to demonstrate adequate yearly progress (AYP) have contributed to the need to more closely monitor student achievement over time in the basic skills areas. In addition, NCLB requires schools to provide more levels or intensity of intervention for students who do not meet benchmarks, or minimal standards. Both of these points are critical components of an RTI system. Adequate yearly progress has now become the evaluative currency on which schools are judged. A school cannot demonstrate AYP unless all students, including disaggregated groups at each grade level, meet designated benchmarks. Schools that are not meeting AYP often begin to focus on schoolwide improvement, typically including implementing an RTI system.

Individuals with Disabilities Education Improvement Act

The Individuals with Disabilities Education Improvement Act (IDEIA) of 2004 represented a reauthorization of the 1997 Individuals with Disabilities Education Act (IDEA). The most recent reauthorization was made to mirror the themes in NCLB that were previously applied only to students with disabilities. These themes include the following mandated points:

◻ All children with disabilities must be included in annual state assessments.

◻ Before referral of a student for special education, his or her parents must be informed of the results of repeated assessments of the student's performance.

◻ Documentation proving that students were exposed to scientifically or evidence-based instruction in the basic skills areas of reading and math before eligibility for special education was determined.

◻ Students found eligible for special education must have the characteristics of a disability, demonstrate a gap in performance due to this disability, and have a documented need for service.

◻ Local educational agencies can use an RTI approach to determine eligibility for special education.

◻ Schools can provide increased intensity of interventions as part of general education.

◻ Districts are allowed to use up to 15 percent of their IDEA funds for these purposes.

The accountability movement growing out of the NCLB and IDEA represents companion laws that address closing the achievement gap between children from the majority group and those from historically low-achieving minority groups. Together those acts underscore the importance of high-quality, scientifically based instructional methods, curricular materials, and intervention strategies; early identification of learning problems; continual monitoring of the impact of instruction; design and implementation of individualized tiered interventions; and inclusion of all students in one accountability system. Finally, they each hold schools accountable for the progress of all students, including those from disaggregated groups, through the documentation of student outcomes using AYP measures.

Scholarly Work Rationale: RTI Is About Evidence-Based Practice

The RTI concept grew out of multiple areas of work in behavioral psychology. These areas included curriculum-based measurement, assessment, and evaluation (Deno, 1985), Positive Behavioral Interventions and Supports (PBIS; Sugai & Horner, 2006), behavioral consultation (Bergan & Kratochwill, 1990), and both laboratory and applied research on behavioral resistance to change (e.g., Fuchs, Fuchs, & Speece, 2002; Gresham, 2002; Herrnstein, 1961).

Bergan and Kratochwill (1990) outlined a process known as systematic behavioral consultation in the 1980s. Their four-stage model of consultation included a final plan evaluation stage in which the consultant assesses the client's response to the intervention as a way to determine "next steps." These "next steps" might include terminating, continuing, or changing the intervention. Sugai and Horner (2006) provided a framework for a comprehensive three-tiered plan (PBIS) that focused on schoolwide intervention support. Gresham (2002) later introduced the concept related to eligibility for special education for students who were thought to be exhibiting characteristics of behavior disorders. This applied work can be traced back to the basic research with laboratory animals whose behavior was resistant to extinction (e.g., Herrnstein, 1961). This "resistance" to intervention has subsequently been adapted to fit a three-tiered system of support similar to that proposed by Sugai and Horner.

As part of the accountability movement, RTI principles have been applied to maximize the educational achievement of all students. The references at the end of this chapter include some seminal works in the field that were instrumental in the development of RTI, in addition to empirical evidence supporting the implementation of RTI for student social behavior and academic performance.

A COMPREHENSIVE, TIERED SYSTEM OF SUPPORT

RTI is often represented as a tiered system of educational service delivery. In this book, we discuss a comprehensive model that addresses both academic performance and social behavior systems, and we discuss how these two systems can be integrated. In addition, we address the slight variations in implementation for consideration by schools with high percentages of unique populations such as English language learners, those enrolled in special education, and students from low-income families. It should be noted that the comprehensive model is the same for these unique populations as for the general school population.

Figure 1.1 depicts a three-tiered comprehensive system of support. Each tier is a unique level of assessment, intervention, and involvement.

FIGURE 1.1   A three-tiered comprehensive system of support.

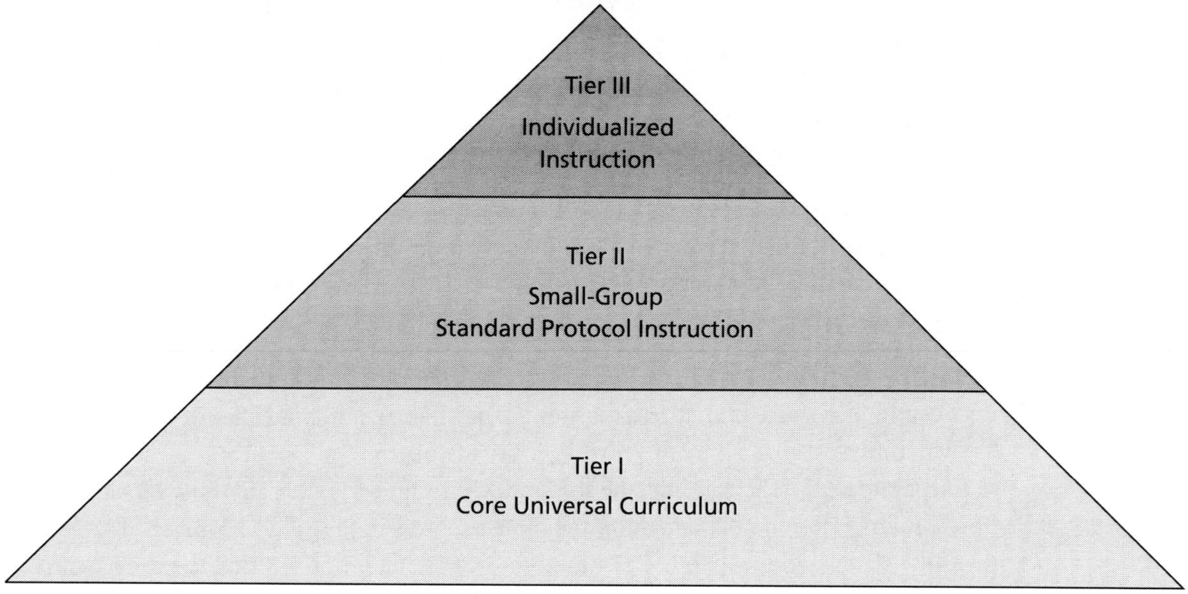

We will now focus on describing general assessment and intervention at each of the three tiers.

What Does a Tier Really Represent?

In this tiered model, all students are provided with the appropriate amount of intervention or instruction necessary for academic and behavioral success. As is sometimes popularly discussed in schools just beginning to implement RTI, tiers do not exist as places. Tiers more accurately represent major points on a continuum of student educational support. This fact is often overlooked by school personnel initially learning about RTI. It is critical for educators to acknowledge that students exist on this continuum. Therefore, the first goal is to determine where each student is on the continuum of academic and social behavior development in order to move to the next goal of providing the necessary support for his or her particular point on the continuum.

In a school that is implementing RTI effectively, a series of assessments to match the various tiers is used. These assessment instruments differ depending on the tier. They are referred to as screeners, diagnostic tools, and progress monitoring instruments. Instruments used are different for academic and social behavior systems. The purpose of this section is to provide an understanding of what a comprehensive RTI assessment and continuum of instruction and support process would look like (as illustrated in Figure 1.1). The details of each of these critical features are described throughout the book.

How Tiers Work

Three things happen as students progress from tier to tier:

- First, the student is provided with an assessment that moves from a brief screening to a targeted standard protocol assessment to a more intensive individualized assessment.

- Second, the student is provided with interventions that move from a universal grade-level curriculum to a targeted standard protocol intervention to a more intensive individualized intervention. These interventions are determined based on the assessments provided at each tier.

- Third, the student is provided with more time and resources to address his or her respective academic or social behavior deficits. Students who receive Tier III individualized services also are provided with Tier II standard protocol services and Tier I universal services.

Figure 1.2 represents a three-tiered system of support conceptualized as a continuum of educational service in mathematics for a hypothetical student. The continuum cannot be overemphasized and is realized when students begin to perform somewhere between two separate tiers—for example, the student, who, after receiving Tier I universal instruction in math, is found not be making adequate progress in the fall. Her universal screening measure (discussed in Chapter 2) in math indicates she is not meeting the progress to be expected based on grade-level criterion. A school implementing a comprehensive RTI framework would be prepared for this situation. After diagnosing the student's strength and weaknesses, they would provide her with a Tier II standard protocol (i.e., evidence-based, scripted, small group, targeted skill) intervention. During winter, the intervention is provided consistently, and the student begins to demonstrate adequate performance by spring. She therefore may no longer need the full specified amount of time of the standard protocol in the late spring, which would allow for a reduction in the amount or intensity of intervention provided. This is commonly referred to as "fading out Tier II intervention." This fading-out can occur at both Tier II and Tier III, but students always receive these services in addition to the core curriculum and instruction for academic performance and social behavior.

Three points should be made about the continuum of support in a comprehensive RTI model. First, because intervention intensity can be faded out, it is possible to have multiple students receive services at the Tier II level but at varying levels of intensity. While one student may be receiving reading instruction for 30 minutes per day three times a week, a second student may need only 30 minutes of instruction two times a week. How this need is determined is explained in Chapter 4 and involves data-based decision making. Second, students may receive differentiated instruction along the continuum. That is, while student A may be receiving reading instruction in phonemic awareness, student B may be receiving reading instruction focusing on building fluency. Similarly, different students in a school may be receiving different social behavior interventions. A student may receive group-administered social skills training to increase assertiveness and friendship-building skills, while another student receives an intervention focused on anger management. Finally, students may be provided one level of service for one area of skill deficit and another level of service for other areas of deficit. For example, because the function of an RTI model is to determine where on the continuum of support a student is for all areas, a student may receive Tier I services only in reading while receiving Tier II-level support for math and social behavior.

FIGURE 1.2   **How tiers work as a continuum of support.**

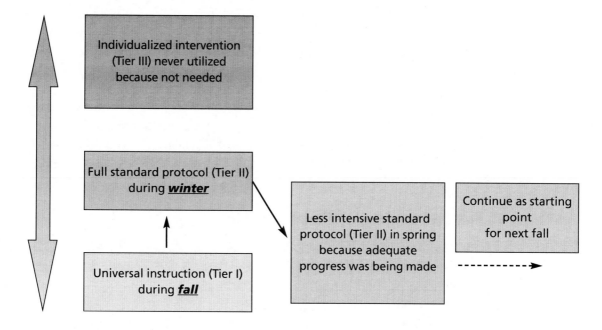

COMPREHENSIVE ASSESSMENT AND INTERVENTION AT TIER I

Tier I: Academic Curriculum and Instruction

Tier I represents what is commonly referred to as the universal curriculum and instruction tier. In education, we refer to it as universal because all students receive it (with modifications for students with severe disabilities). The curriculum is provided to all students and should be effective for the vast majority of students without further intervention. Typically, 80 percent of students demonstrating adequate improvement is considered the rule of thumb when evaluating effectiveness, but it may vary depending on the school or district and current adequate yearly progress standards. A Tier I curriculum must be scientifically based and, when implemented with integrity (as intended by the curriculum developers), adequately address the educational needs of students as evidenced by their performance on high-stakes tests.

Tier I: Screening for Academic Problems

Rather than rely on results of high-stakes testing, which can take an inordinate amount of time to be scored and returned to schools, an RTI model incorporates measurement of student performance for all students three or four times per year. The performance and progress are assessed using a brief (i.e., a few short minutes) universal screening measure described in Chapter 2. This assessment allows educators to efficiently monitor the performance of all students and identify those who may be at risk for not meeting expectations. Educators can therefore provide such students with appropriate targeted instruction much earlier.

Tier I: Social Behavior Curriculum and Instruction

There are various statewide assessments used to evaluate universal curricula for social behavior. Prevention models that follow RTI logic include such programs as PBIS (Sugai & Horner, 2006) and Project ACHIEVE (Knoff, 2009), in which a specific social skills curriculum is used with all children in the school. Typically, training in social skills and instruction about behavioral expectations are provided to all children in a school regardless of student ability (with some modifications made for students with severe disabilities). For example, many schools establish three to five expectations that are taught at various levels of sophistication, depending on grade, to all students. Violations of these expectations are documented, and data from the documentation are analyzed to inform future instruction on specific expectations.

Tier I: Screening for Social Behavior

Unlike academic screening, social behavior screening is not used for monitoring progress but is used solely for the purpose of assessing behavior problems. Typically, behavior screening is not a test of a child's performance on a benchmark; instead, it relies on teacher perceptions and/or recall of critical events that predict future antisocial behavior. Research (e.g., Ollendick, Greene, Weist, & Oswald, 1990) suggests that teacher perceptions are very useful for this purpose, and there are a number of valid screening tools available. We discuss a process and options for screening in Chapter 2.

COMPREHENSIVE ASSESSMENT AND INTERVENTION AT TIER II

Tier II: Educational Diagnostic Tools for Academics

Educational diagnostics have a number of components and represent a process. The process requires more than a simple score on a test to inform an educational decision for students at the Tier II level. Educational diagnostic tools are readily available and are commonly used in schools. They are easy to use and help identify specific educational strengths and weaknesses. It should be pointed out that these strengths and weaknesses focus on specific academic skills (e.g., regrouping in mathematics, letter–sound correspondence) and not on psychological processes (e.g., auditory or visual learning; Shapiro, 2004). These tools are useful because they can help a school pinpoint the type of Tier II intervention needed for students who are not on target for making adequate yearly progress. Educational diagnostic tools and the diagnostic process are described in Chapter 3.

Tier II: Academic Standard Protocol Interventions

Tier II represents what is commonly referred to as the standard protocol tier. This standard protocol of support is provided in addition to the Tier I universal curriculum. Specifically, the standard protocol support is a systematic intervention process designed to target performance of those students who do not make adequate progress within the universal curriculum alone. One way to determine a student's need for services at the Tier II level is to demonstrate a lower rate of improvement in the specified area relative to the student's peers on a universal screening measure. Another way to demonstrate a student's need for services at the Tier II level is to demonstrate a lower level of performance in the specified area relative to a correlation-derived cut score that represents a relationship between the high-stakes assessment outcome measure and the universal screening measure (this is more fully described, and methods compared and contrasted, in Chapter 4). The specific intervention (or interventions—a school would likely provide several to meet diverse needs) provided in a standard protocol is selected based on the results of the administration of an educational diagnostic tool and a review of current instructional practices (an instructional analysis form is provided in the appendix and on the accompanying CD and is discussed more fully in Chapter 3). In a comprehensive model of RTI, it is important that any intervention be matched to identified student needs. It should be noted that assessment and intervention are both more intensive at Tier II than at Tier I. Progress is monitored at least biweekly for students receiving Tier II services, using progress monitoring tools very similar to the universal screening measures used in Tier I. Progress monitoring is addressed in Chapter 4.

Tier II: Social Behavior Assessment

There are several assessment and diagnostic procedures for social behavior available to a school implementing a comprehensive model of RTI. Most frequently, schools have relied on office discipline referrals for making screening decisions. We recommend the use of a system in which students have to meet specific criteria based on screening measures that have been identified as reliable and valid. Schools often use daily behavior reports to closely monitor progress of these students in combination with other broad indicators such as office discipline referrals and tardiness records. We discuss the application and use of Tier II assessment for social behavior in Chapter 3.

Tier II: Social Behavior Standard Protocol Interventions

Like their counterpart in academics, social behavior interventions in a comprehensive RTI model are typically standard protocol. They include an intervention targeted at a broad array of social behavior problems. This type of intervention approach is more likely to be effective if the intervention is implemented early, before the problem has become intense. The interventions are typically easy for a school to implement, but they do require monitoring and some problem solving. One common example is check-in/check-out systems. For this intervention, there is a scripted procedure (i.e., a standard protocol) whereby students check in with a teacher at a given time period and check out at the end of a period (the procedure varies depending on the educational level of the student). During the check-in time, students are reminded what is expected of them; during check-out time, their performance, recorded on a behavior report card, is discussed. Consistent successes are reinforced at an established criteria level for success. Some comprehensive RTI schools prefer more-specific social skills that also have a specific programmed and sequenced curriculum.

COMPREHENSIVE ASSESSMENT AND INTERVENTION AT TIER III

Tier III: Individualized Academic Assessment

The intervention that is provided as part of an individualized instruction is selected based on the outcome of a curriculum-based evaluation (CBE). CBE focuses on analyzing student responses to academic tasks and then developing and testing hypotheses. Curriculum-based evaluation methods will be more fully discussed in Chapter 3.

Tier III: Individualized Academic Instruction and Support

Tier III represents what is commonly referred to as individualized instruction. This individualized instruction is provided in addition to the Tier II standard protocol and Tier I universal instruction. Specifically, the individualized intervention is designed for students who, despite the Tier I universal curriculum and Tier II standard protocol intervention, are not making adequate rates of improvement toward meeting standards as measured by high-stakes assessments. It should be noted that both assessment and intervention are more intensive at Tier III than at Tier II and Tier I. Progress is monitored one or more times per week for students receiving Tier III services, using tools similar to the universal screening measures used in Tiers I and II.

Tier III: Social Behavior Assessment

Functional behavior assessment (FBA) and functional analysis (FA) are effective procedures for identifying effective interventions for individual students. FBA uses systematic data collection methods that involve a series of steps during which educators identify the antecedent, behavior, and consequences of behavior problems in a descriptive fashion. FA is a systematic method of experimentally manipulating the classroom environment to directly test hypotheses related to the conditions that may evoke or maintain the problem behavior. There are a variety of approaches to FBA and FA, from simple interviews to complex analytical procedures, available for schools implementing a comprehensive RTI process.

Tier III: Social Behavior Interventions

Multicomponent positive behavior support plans are the most effective and useful interventions for students who need the intensive support of Tier III. In this model, scientific, research-based interventions are used to support students across antecedent, behavior, and reinforcing consequences identified through the FBA process. Teaching new skills to replace maladaptive behavior and to encourage positive preventive strategies is emphasized. Matching intervention strategies to the findings of the FBA is a critical part of the process. Support for students is more intense at Tier III; however, the preventive interventions and instruction at Tiers I and II are designed to keep schools from having an overabundance of students who need Tier III support.

It should be reiterated that students receiving services at a given tier (e.g., Tier III) also receive instruction at the level of lower-level tiers (e.g., Tier II and Tier I). Again, we emphasize that tiers are not places but are points in a continuum of service delivery.

RESPONSE TO INTERVENTION AS A DATA-BASED DECISION-MAKING PROCESS

The following are all important determinations to be made within a comprehensive RTI system:

◻ How frequently to assess student performance

◻ What assessments to use

◻ What interventions to choose

◻ How long to intervene at a given tier

◻ When to fade an intervention

◻ When to intensify services

◻ When to consider special education entitlement

A major focus of this book, therefore, is to provide a framework for making each of the decisions using data in a systematic way for all students, and which is consistent, objective, and focused on helping students meet educational standards. Figure 1.3 is a general flowchart of the entire process of a comprehensive RTI model. Each shape represents an area for which data-based decision making is required. Each area is addressed in the book, in the order shown on the flowchart. Squares represent instruction, triangles represent assessment, diamond shapes represent progress monitoring, and circles represent an important consideration, identifying at-risk students, which we focus on in-depth in Chapter 2.

SUMMARY OF IMPORTANT POINTS

This chapter provides a foundation of what RTI is and how it might be implemented within a school. After reading this chapter, you are encouraged to study the final chapter of this book. The final chapter addresses important considerations and lessons learned, which you are likely to find helpful in understanding and navigating the challenges that come with the implementation of RTI.

The following are important points of RTI to be stressed to anyone you may be working with in the early stages of implementation.

◻ **RTI focuses on the educational needs of all children.** RTI is a model of service delivery that focuses on identifying the educational needs of all students and is not exclusively focused on special education, general education, or at-risk students.

◻ **RTI is prevention, as opposed to reaction, oriented.** Because RTI emphasizes the screening of student performance three times per year, it can allow educators to identify students who are beginning to make less progress compared to their peers.

◻ **RTI relies primarily on empirical data for decision making.** RTI focuses on making decisions related to educational need for all students, using systematic data collection and analysis as it relates to the prediction of outcomes on high-stakes testing.

◻ **RTI focuses on implementation of empirically supported, scientifically based instruction and intervention.** A hallmark of RTI models is the use of only those practices for which data are available to support their implementation. This is the case for both academic performance and social behavior interventions across all tiers.

FIGURE 1.3   **General flowchart for the RTI process.**

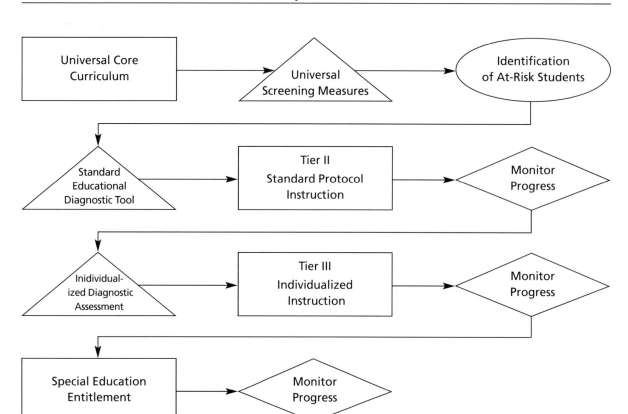

□ **RTI utilizes only those assessment approaches that have instructional value.** RTI encourages the use of assessment tools that are useful for informing the next level of assessment and/or instruction, and it discourages use of assessment methods that are not informative to instructional programming.

□ **RTI emphasizes that tiers are not places.** Tiers are major markers on a continuum of educational service delivery. Students at the same major marker on a continuum may not receive the same amount of instructional support. One student may require 30 minutes three times per week of additional Tier II support, while another who has been successful with that amount may begin to be faded to two times per week or less.

□ **RTI services are dynamic.** Students may be at a specific point on the continuum of educational service delivery for long periods of time. The key is to find at what point on the continuum each student is successful.

□ **RTI acknowledges that intra-individual needs in instructional support are likely.** Students who are at a specific point on the continuum of service for one subject may be at a different point on the continuum for other subjects. It is possible for a student to receive Tier III services for reading, Tier II support for mathematics, and Tier I support for behavior.

REFERENCES

Bergan, J. R., & Kratochwill, T. R. (1990). *Behavioral consultation and therapy.* New York, NY: Plenum.

Deno, S. L. (1985). Curriculum-based measurement: The emerging alternative. *Exceptional Children, 52,* 219–232.

Fuchs, L. S., Fuchs, D., & Speece, D.L. (2002). Treatment validity as a unifying construct for identifying learning disabilities. *Learning Disability Quarterly, 25,* 33–45.

Gresham, F. M. (2002). Responsiveness to intervention: An alternative approach to the identification of learning disabilities. In R. Bradley, L. Danielson, & D.P. Hallahan (Eds.), *Identification of learning disabilities: Research to practice* (pp. 467–519). Mahwah, NJ: Erlbaum.

Herrnstein, R. J. (1961). Relative and absolute strength of responses as a function of frequency of reinforcement. *Journal of the Experimental Analysis of Behavior, 4,* 267–272.

Individuals with Disabilities Education Act, Pub. L. No. 105–17 (1997).

Individuals with Disabilities Education Improvement Act, Pub. L. No. 108–446 (2004).

Knoff, H. (2009). Project Achieve. www.projectachieve.info/home.html

No Child Left Behind Act, Pub. L. No. 107–110 (2001).

Ollendick, T. H., Greene, R., Weist, M. D., and Oswald D. P. (1990). The predicitive validity of teacher nominations: A five-year followup of at-risk youth. *Journal of Abnormal Psychology, 18,* 699–713.

Shapiro, E. (2004). *Academic skills problems: Direct assessment and intervention* (3rd ed.). New York, NY: Guilford Press.

Sugai, G., & Horner, R. (2006). A promising approach for expanding and sustaining school-wide positive behavior support. *School Psychology Review, 35,* 245–259.

RECOMMENDED RESOURCES

Individuals with Disabilities Education Improvement Act

http://idea.ed.gov

National Center on Response to Intervention

www.rti4success.org

No Child Left Behind Act (Overview)

www2.ed.gov/nclb/overview/intro/edpicks.jhtml?src=ln

Response to Intervention: Policy Considerations and Implementation (2005)

National Association of State Directors of Special Education, Inc.

Alexandria, VA

CHAPTER 2

Universal Screening Measures and Data Analysis for Academic Performance and Social Behavior

CHAPTER OVERVIEW

Universal screening measures (USM) are critical components of RTI. Without a universal screening measure, a school is not fully implementing RTI. This chapter will aid in the understanding of universal screening measures for academic performance and social behavior. This chapter builds on the previous chapter's objectives. Specifically, this chapter will:

- Provide a purpose, rationale, and description of what constitutes a universal screening measure for academic performance (USM-A) and social behavior (USM-B).

- Describe how to make data-based decisions related to the universal screening instrument.

- Discuss how to obtain standards-based cut scores (benchmarks) and why they are preferable to the other two major ways of deriving cut scores.

- Describe how to make data-based decisions with universal screening instruments to identify students at risk for academic performance and social behavior problems.

PURPOSES OF UNIVERSAL SCREENING MEASURES

The purpose of a universal screening measure is two-fold: (1) to predict which students may have difficulty passing the high-stakes test that is used in a particular school district's state, and (2) to monitor progress over time of all students in developing academic or behavior skills. A universal screening measure should be used for reading, mathematics, written expression, and behavior.

RATIONALE FOR UNIVERSAL SCREENING MEASURES

Universal screening measures are similar to a medical checkup in that they are good predictors of overall academic and behavioral health. It should be noted that these indicators do not identify the intervention or treatment that is needed for better academic or behavioral performance. Intervention or treatment development requires a more time-intensive diagnostic assessment and is described in the next chapter. The indicators should, however, serve as useful gauges of overall academic performance and behavioral health and are similar to blood pressure, heart rate, respiration, body temperature, and weight as indicators of physical health.

In reading, for example, indicators such as how fast a student reads (oral reading fluency), how many letters a student can identify in a minute (letter naming fluency), how many digits he or she can calculate in a minute (computation fluency), and how many word sequences he or she can string together when writing a short story (writing fluency) can provide a picture of overall academic health. Teacher ratings of particular behaviors or student behavioral outcomes, such as the number of referrals to the office, can provide a picture of overall behavioral health. If a student's performance is not in line with developmental milestones (i.e., benchmarks) and trajectories, then intervention may be warranted.

CHARACTERISTICS OF UNIVERSAL SCREENING MEASURES

A universal screening instrument should do all of the following:

▫ Be brief to administer.

▫ Allow for multiple administrations and repeated measurement of student performance each year.

▫ Be simple to score and interpret.

▫ Reduce the number of students needing diagnostic assessment (as discussed in the next chapter).

▫ Predict academic performance on high-stakes tests or identify possibly serious behavioral concerns.

Predicting Academic Performance on High-Stakes Tests

Being able to predict the future is powerful. Being able to predict specifically which students will meet and not meet standards on high-stakes testing is advantageous to any school district. Having an accurate prediction of students who may fail to meet mandated standards affords schools the opportunity to provide systematic universal instruction to all (Tier I) or interventions (at Tiers II and III) aimed at preventing such academic failure. Correlation is a statistical term that describes a predictive relationship between two variables—for example, between a student's results from a universal screening and that student's later performance on a high-stakes test. A correlation tells us the strength and direction of the relationship between two variables. The strength of the relationship ranges from 0 to 1. The closer to 1, the stronger (or more predictable) the relationship, while 0 represents the absence of any relationship or predictability. The direction of the relationship can be either positive or negative. A positive relationship indicates that as one variable goes up, the other also is likely to go up; a negative correlation indicates that as one variable goes up or down, the other variable is likely to do the opposite.

In the case of predicting high-stakes testing scores, it is desirable to have a universal screening instrument that correlates strongly and positively to test performance. That is, we want a correlation between our universal screening instrument and high-stakes outcome to approach 1 as closely as possible. The extent to which we know the correlation between a universal screening instrument and high-stakes testing performance affects how confident we can be in identifying students at risk for failing to meet academic standards and thus help us provide interventions aimed at preventing such failure.

It should be pointed out that no perfect prediction is possible with a universal screening instrument. That is, some students will do better than predicted, while others will do worse than predicted on the criterion (i.e., the high-stakes test). It is therefore important to know not only the correlation of the two instruments but also the proportion of students who are accurately and inaccurately identified. Discussion related to correlations and accurate identification is more fully addressed in Chapter 4.

Brief Time for Administration and Training

Although accurately predicting student performance on high-stakes tests through a universal screening measure is helpful, its use should not be unwieldy. The administration of the measure should require minimal time. For example, a screening instrument that requires 30 minutes to administer to each student independently will require approximately 10 to 12 hours to administer to an entire classroom of 20 to 25 students. This amount of time equates to approximately more than a full week of instructional time (6 school days), which could be spent instead on preventive or remedial instruction with students.

Therefore, it is important to use a universal screening tool that not only can predict high-stakes testing outcomes well but also can be administered in the classroom by the teacher in a short period of time (just a few minutes), either to individual students or, even better, to a group. In addition, learning to administer a universal screening instrument should not require a large amount of training. The key is to be simple and brief. If training to learn administration and scoring procedures takes more than a day of in-service training, there may be some need to consider the cost of such a procedure.

Easy Scoring and Interpretation

Because all students will be evaluated by the universal screening tool, it is important that the amount of time to score the instrument be limited. It is helpful to have an instrument for which the scoring is conducted during the administration. Today, some universal screening instruments have electronic scoring devices that also facilitate data entry into data management software.

Equally important is the ease of data interpretation. Because the function of a universal screening instrument is to quickly identify students who may be at risk for not meeting standards on high-stakes tests, the interpretation of the data should be limited to such a decision. The interpretation should not focus on educational placement or type of instruction. In addition, the results should be easily explainable to all stakeholders, including students and their parents or guardians.

Multiple Administrations and Repeated Measurement of Student Performance

Response to Intervention focuses on prevention of academic skills deficits. Therefore, it is important to monitor the progress of all students over time and evaluate the extent to which any student may be falling off pace with peers. By doing so, educators can make decisions at various points in the year about the best way to maintain or improve educational performance of all students.

To make such an educational decision, at least three data points are required. Three data points allow a decision maker to form conclusions related to the trend of a student's data (more fully described in Chapter 4). However, the point to be made here is that because three data points are required to make a decision, a sufficient number (at least three) of alternate forms of the universal screening instrument should be available.

Reducing the Need for Diagnostic Assessment

It is important to reiterate that a universal screening instrument is *not* a diagnostic tool (see Chapter 3). One of the primary objectives of the universal screening instrument is to minimize the number of students who need to be further assessed using an educational diagnostic tool. This provides more time for diagnostic assessment of students who are more likely to benefit from it, allowing educators to use the capitalized time to provide needed interventions to students.

UNIVERSAL SCREENING MEASURES FOR ACADEMIC PERFORMANCE (USM-A)

Universal screening measures for academic performance (USM-A) are readily available commercially or can be constructed from a school's curricular materials. USM-A are often referred to as curriculum-based measurements (CBM) because they utilize direct measurement of student response to a leveled curriculum (preferably one that the student is being instructed in at grade level). CBMs have many of the same characteristics as USM-A, but they have a few more characteristics, which are discussed in Chapter 4.

Reading

There are a number of USM-A recommended for reading. However, what is recommended for a given grade level is based on the development of reading skills. The National Reading Panel (National Institute of Child Health and Human Development, 2000) suggests the five major areas of reading: phonemic awareness, phonics, fluency, vocabulary, and comprehension. Each of these areas may be best screened with different measures.

Phonemic Awareness

Phonemic awareness is the ability to identify the smallest units of sound in words. Phonemic awareness is generally screened through tasks similar to phoneme segmentation—that is, presenting a student with a list of words orally and having him or her tell you the sounds (the phonemes) in the word. For example, the screening administrator says *cat,* and the student is required to say *k, a,* and *t* to correctly identify the three phonemes. These types of screenings are typically done at the kindergarten level.

Phonics

Phonics ability demonstrates an understanding of letter and sound correspondence. Phonics ability is generally screened through tasks similar to nonsense word fluency—that is, presenting a list of printed words that are not real words (e.g., *vop, dak, tiv*) and asking the student to read as many as he or she can in a short, specified period of time. These screenings are typically done at the kindergarten or first-grade level.

Fluency

Oral reading fluency is traditionally assessed by listening to a student read a grade-level passage aloud for 1 minute. Oral reading fluency is measured by the number of words read correctly per minute (WRC). This is accomplished by the teacher following along with his or her own copy of the passage and marking each word the student misses. Then, by subtracting the number of words missed from the number of total words read, the teacher calculates the oral reading fluency score. The WRC measure has been found to be a very strong predictor of reading competence (Fuchs, Fuchs, Hosp, & Jenkins, 2001). It is generally not recommended to begin administering these measures until about first grade, and it is suggested that they continue to be administered as screening tools throughout the elementary school years.

Vocabulary and Comprehension

Vocabulary and comprehension are tricky constructs of reading ability to screen. This is because many variables affect comprehension, including background knowledge, motivation, and reading fluency. For example, multiple procedures are available for screening comprehension, such as Maze, Cloze, and True–False. However, when these procedures are empirically investigated, they are found to be measuring essentially the same dimension of reading as oral reading fluency. Maze, for example, is a procedure that is presented to all children at the same time in a group format. Students are given a short passage to read. The passage has, on average, every seventh word omitted. Students have 3 minutes to work on as much of the passage as possible and are required to choose the best word (from among three) that makes the most sense in completing the passage. An inherent problem here is guessing, which allows a correct response one third of the time by chance. A student could randomly choose answers and get a total score of 20 correct out of 60, while another student who reads slowly and carefully might get 20 correct out of 20 attempts. Both students are seen as equally accurate in their respective "comprehension."

Another procedure, Cloze, is essentially identical to Maze, except it is fill in the blank rather than multiple choice. Finally, comprehension may be assessed through true and false measures. These measures essentially provide students with statements that are well known, such as "The sky is blue," and the student is required to circle either true or false as the answer. In our own unpublished research, attempts of using true and false items yielded similar results and challenges as Cloze procedures do. At this time, there is no known measure better than oral reading fluency for assessing reading comprehension that is brief, predictive of future reading outcomes, and easy to score.

Written Expression

Written expression is usually assessed with story starters. Story starters are simple sentence fragments that prompt students to write creatively. For example, students may be given the story starter, "If I could be granted one wish, I …" Students are allowed a specified period of time (such as 1 minute) to think about what to write and then a specified time (such as 3 minutes) to write. The amount of time is not important. However, the time should be consistent across all students and all test administrations to ensure that reliable decisions can made at the time of data analysis. Also, the time periods should be brief. Although students should be allowed enough time to begin writing their stories, it is not important that they finish. The story starter is efficient because it allows for whole-class administration in about 4 minutes.

Words Written Correctly and Total Word Sequences

The primary variable of interest when scoring story starters is the number of words written correctly. This is calculated by simply counting up the number of total words written and spelled correctly. Total word sequences is another variable that can be used in the data-based decision-making process. It is calculated by counting the number of words that are appropriately sequenced in sentences.

Spelling

Spelling is usually screened through a classwide administration of a spelling probe. Spelling probes consist of a specified number (such as 15) of grade-level spelling words presented at a specified pace (such as 7 seconds). The test administrator says each word, uses it in a sentence, and says it again. Students spell the words on a sheet of notebook paper. Spelling probes such as these are very quick to administer because they are presented in a class-wide format.

Correct Letter Sequences

To score spelling probes, the teacher sums the number of correct letter sequences. A correct letter sequence (CLS) is defined as any sequence of two letters or a letter and space (i.e., not putting a letter where one shouldn't be) for which the spelling is accurate for a specified word. For example, the word *boy* has four CLSs: (1) space to *b,* (2) *b* to *o,* (3) *o* to *y,* and (4) *y* to space. If, for example, a student spelled *boy* as *bay,* the student would earn two CLSs. The space to *b* sequence is correct and so is the *y* to space sequence.

   This scoring procedure is helpful for two reasons. First, it allows for more-sensitive monitoring of progress. Students who come close to spelling the words correctly are not as "severe" as students who do not come close to spelling the words correctly. Second, it may allow for a pattern analysis by the teacher. A teacher may recognize that a student consistently missed spelling sequences containing silent *e,* or made a consistent error with a specific vowel sequence. These patterns may facilitate an understanding of what type of intervention may be needed, especially at the individual Tier III level of support.

Mathematics

Mathematics screening instruments have generally focused on early numeracy and computation. Increasingly, tool developers (see, for example, AIMSweb.com and easyCBM.com) are providing math application measures. In addition, some newer tools (such as easyCBM®) allow screening in higher-order skills such as algebra and geometry. For all of these variables, a student is generally provided with a probe (i.e., worksheet) and required to work as many of the problems as quickly and accurately as possible within a specified time limit. Sometimes, as with easyCBM, students can take the tests online.

Digits Correct per Minute

Students can receive partial credit with the digits correct per minute (DCM) method. That is, if a student responded "24" to the problem $10 + 14 = ?$, he or she would be awarded two DCM (one for each digit, 2 and 4). However, a response of "14" would earn one DCM because the student provided just one correct digit. This method is used in curriculum-based measurement procedures because it allows for more-sensitive measurement of student performance (Deno, 1989).

Accuracy

Student performance on some measures, such as math applications, is simply scored as correct or incorrect, and students get a raw score and/or accuracy percentage.

DATA-BASED DECISION MAKING USING UNIVERSAL SCREENING MEASURES FOR ACADEMIC PERFORMANCE

Because a universal screening measure is crucial to the identification of students who may be at risk for failing to meet expectations on high-stakes assessments, it is important to ensure that the chosen universal screening measure is reliable and valid. A reliable and valid universal screening measure is one that will predict high-stakes testing scores and consistently identify students who have a high probability of not meeting expectations, such as the adequate yearly progress (AYP) standards established by the No Child Left Behind Act.

Students who do not meet specified criteria are identified as students at risk. The criteria, or benchmarks, used for deciding which students are at risk can have differential effects on which students are identified. There are three general ways of making this decision. Specifically, data analyzers can compare a student's current performance to that of his or her peers; they can compare a student's current rate of improvement to that of his or her peers; or they can predict a student's future performance relative to a standard (such as AYP) based on his or her current performance.

Percentile Rank Approach

The percentile rank approach compares a student's current level of performance to that of his or her peers. The rationale is simple: Any student scoring at or below a given percentile rank (e.g., 25th percentile or 15th percentile) is considered at risk. The advantages to this model are that it is simple to understand and easily computed and analyzed. Figure 2.1 is an example of a sampling list of students sorted by percentile rank on a universal screening measure of oral reading fluency.

Students are ranked by the number of words read correctly (WRC) per minute. This allows for a very quick and easy referencing of all students in a hierarchical manner. Despite these advantages, the percentile rank option does not allow for any link to high-stakes testing and achieving AYP. Moreover, it is possible that a student's score at School A is at the 25th percentile but when compared to students at School B, that same student is at the 75th percentile. In this scenario, the student may receive additional Tier II support in School A but not in School B. Likewise, if the student receives services in School A and performance increases for all students (including the at-risk student), he or she could still be at the 25th percentile and considered at risk—although not actually at risk for anything related to AYP. The bottom line is not how well students perform compared to their peers but how well students perform relative to imposed standards.

It should be pointed out that the percentile rank approach is often applied to national norms. That is, instead of comparing students to their own peers, student performance is compared to a larger national sample such as those available through AIMSweb, easyCBM, and the DIBELS Data System®. Because the norms at those sources are not necessarily tied to AYP, the same problem exists—namely, that a student can score relatively high or low, but there is no indication of whether the student is on track to make AYP.

Dual Discrepancy Approach

Because an assessment based on a single point in time (such as a percentile rank) has its limitations, it may be argued that it is important to consider multiple points in time. The logic here is also fairly simple: Monitor student progress over time and compare rates of improvement (learning trajectories) to those of peers. If instruction is effective, we should see improvement in student performance over time relative to peers. To be accurately identified as needing more-intensive and more-frequent instruction, a student should demonstrate a dual discrepancy. That is, a student should be discrepant (below average or some other percentile) from peers *and* this discrepancy should be increasing over time (the gap is becoming wider).

Figure 2.2 is an example of dual discrepancy for a student named William. William is discrepant (below average) at benchmarking period 1. This below-average performance is not sufficient by itself, however, to suggest that William needs additional instructional intervention because, in most instances, half of students fall above the average while the other half fall below it, and providing additional instructional services to half the school population is not an efficient use of educational resources. However, at benchmarking period 2, it is clear that the gap between William's performance and that of his peers is becoming larger. At this point, William would be a likely candidate for increased intensity of instructional services.

FIGURE 2.1   **Example of a sampling of student performance, ordered by and based on percentile ranks.**

Student	Teacher	Fall WRC	Winter WRC	Winter Percentile Rank	Level	
A, B	Adams	209	208	1.00	Well Above Average	**TIER I**
B, C	Brady	159	170	0.93	Well Above Average	
C, D	Adams	134	156	0.90	Above Average	
D, E	Adams	130	148	0.81	Above Average	
E, F	Adams	115	145	0.75	Average	
F, G	Brady	96	133	0.68	Average	
G, H	Brady	109	114	0.51	Average	
H, I	Condon	66	112	0.46	Average	
I, J	Condon	92	94	0.36	Average	
J, K	Condon	61	80	0.25	Average	
K, L	Adams	39	65	0.24	Below Average	**TIER II**
L, M	Condon	42	63	0.22	Below Average	
M, N	Brady	50	60	0.20	Below Average	
N, O	Brady	28	58	0.19	Below Average	
O, P	Adams	20	54	0.17	Below Average	
P, Q	Adams	38	51	0.15	Below Average	
Q, R	Brady	47	48	0.14	Below Average	
R, S	Adams	47	45	0.10	Below Average	
S, T	Condon	38	45	0.10	Below Average	
T, U	Brady	42	41	0.08	Well Below Average	**TIER III**
U, V	Condon	31	39	0.07	Well Below Average	
V, W	Adams	30	38	0.03	Well Below Average	
W, X	Brady	18	38	0.03	Well Below Average	
X, Y	Condon	8	21	0.02	Well Below Average	
Y, Z	Brady	7	18	0.00	Well Below Average	

Let's revisit the percentile approach relative to the dual discrepancy approach. Figure 2.3 is a ranking of students based on percentile ranks (as in Figure 2.1). However, two additional data fields have been added: average rate of improvement (average number of words gained per week) and student rate of improvement (how much gain was made on average per week by each student).

Notice that three students actually performed lower in the winter than in the fall. This results in a negative rate of progress. Others, however, not only made positive gains in performance but also surpassed the average rate of progress (1.3, shown in the next to last column). The dual discrepancy approach identifies students who are below average *and* whose rate of progress is below the average rate of progress. These are the students who are falling behind their peers. We are not simply concerned about the below-average students. Someone must always be last. Being last in a particular group does not mean that the student is destined to be left behind or is even a concern. The student is simply the lowest in that group. The same student could well be the highest performer in another school.

FIGURE 2.2   **Example of a dual discrepancy approach.**

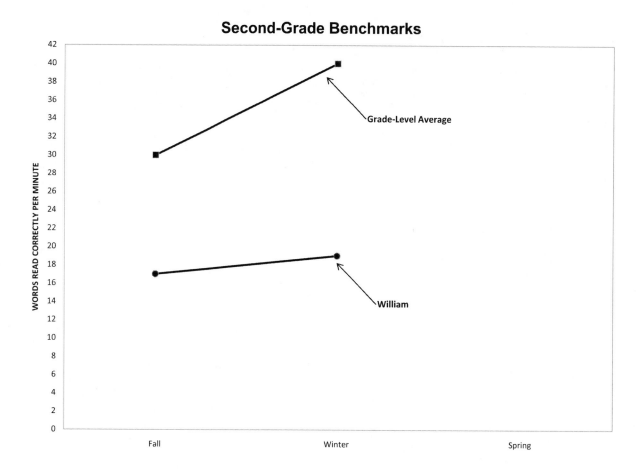

Although the dual discrepancy approach considers student performance over time relative to peers, it does not focus on the importance of knowing whether the student is likely to make AYP. The standards-based prediction approach addresses that limitation.

Standards-Based Prediction Approach

It should be apparent that we as educators would like to predict which students will not make AYP so that we can provide intervention services to help prevent this failure. To make this prediction, we use a statistical procedure called a correlation (as previously defined and discussed). By calculating a correlation, we can better understand what a student with score X on the universal screening measure is likely to attain (e.g., score Y) on a high-stakes test. Because the high-stakes test delineates what constitutes "meets expectations" in AYP and what does not, we can predict which students are unlikely to meet such expectations.

ESTABLISHING BENCHMARKS FOR A STANDARDS-BASED APPROACH

To predict student performance, data from a universal screening measure must be obtained. These data can be entered into a spreadsheet along with subsequent high-stakes test results and correlations calculated. By calculating the slope and *y*-intercept of those two variables, we can determine the level of performance a student needs to reach to have a

FIGURE 2.3   **Example of student performance, ordered by and based on percentile ranks, with rate of progress considered.**

Student	Teacher	Fall WRC	Winter WRC	Winter Percentile Rank	Rate of Improvement	Average Rate of Improvement	Level	
A, b	Adams	209	208	1.00	−0.1	1.3	Well Above Average	
B, C	Brady	159	170	0.93	0.6	1.3	Well Above Average	
C, D	Condon	134	156	0.90	1.2	1.3	Above Average	
D, E	Adams	130	148	0.81	1.0	1.3	Above Average	
E, F	Adams	115	145	0.75	1.7	1.3	Average	TIER I
F, G	Brady	96	133	0.68	2.1	1.3	Average	
G, H	Brady	109	114	0.51	0.3	1.3	Average	
H, I	Condon	66	112	0.46	2.6	1.3	Average	
I, J	Condon	92	94	0.36	0.1	1.3	Average	
J, K	Condon	61	80	0.25	1.1	1.3	Average	
K, L	Adams	39	65	0.24	1.4	1.3	Below Average	
L, M	Condon	42	63	0.22	1.2	1.3	Below Average	
M, N	Brady	50	60	0.20	0.6	1.3	Below Average	
N, O	Brady	28	58	0.19	1.7	1.3	Below Average	
O, P	Adams	20	54	0.17	1.9	1.3	Below Average	TIER II
P, Q	Adams	38	51	0.15	0.7	1.3	Below Average	
Q, R	Brady	47	48	0.14	0.1	1.3	Below Average	
R, S	Adams	47	45	0.10	−0.1	1.3	Below Average	
S, T,	Condon	38	45	0.10	0.4	1.3	Below Average	
T, U	Brady	42	41	0.08	−0.1	1.3	Well Below Average	
U, V	Condon	31	39	0.07	0.4	1.3	Well Below Average	
V, W	Adams	30	38	0.03	0.4	1.3	Well Below Average	
W, X	Brady	18	38	0.03	1.1	1.3	Well Below Average	TIER III
X, Y	Condon	8	21	0.02	0.7	1.3	Well Below Average	
Y, Z	Brady	7	18	0.00	0.6	1.3	Well Below Average	

strong probability of attaining the "meets expectations" criterion. Microsoft Excel® allows users to quickly enter data, and the program will calculate correlations based on that data. (Instructions are provided in the appendix and on the accompanying CD.)

Figure 2.4 displays performance data on a high-stakes test in third grade on the *y* (vertical) axis and oral reading fluency scores (words read correctly per minute, WRC) from the second grade for the same group of students on the *x* (horizontal) axis. WRC scores above the thick horizontal line in the center of the figure are those of students who are predicted to meet expectations on the high-stakes test. The thick vertical line represents the score on the universal screening measure at which meeting expectations on the high-stakes test is likely. These data suggest that students who have a high probability of meeting expectations in third grade were reading at least 78 words correct per minute in the fall of second grade.

FIGURE 2.4 **Performance data on a high-stakes test in third grade on the *y* (vertical) axis, and oral reading fluency scores from the second grade for the same group of students on the *x* (horizontal) axis.**

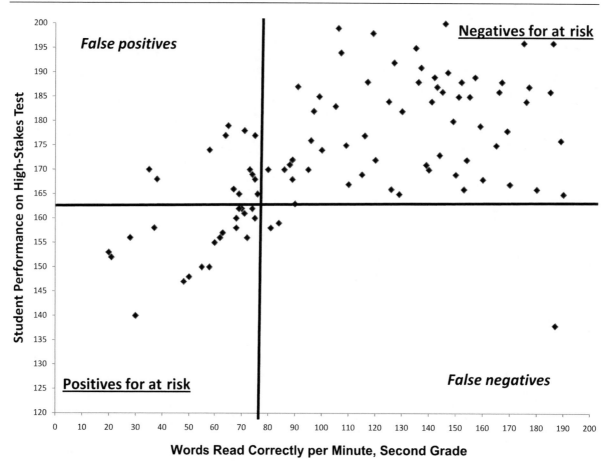

Although we are now able to predict high-stakes testing performance based on a universal screening instrument, the instrument is not perfect. Specifically, two types of errors in prediction are possible: false negatives and false positives.

False Negatives

Note that three students scored below the "meets expectations" benchmark (cut score) but above 78 WRC per minute. These three students are referred to as false negatives. False negatives are a concern because they indicate students not identified for more intensive service who should have been. False negatives can be minimized by attending to predictive validity and extraneous variation. Predictive validity refers to the extent to which the universal screening measure predicts the high-stakes testing performance. To maximize the predictive validity and therefore decrease false negatives (and false positives, explained in the next section), it is important to utilize a universal screening instrument that has a strong correlation with the chosen high-stakes assessment measure. Although an instrument that predicts a perfect correlation does not exist, educational decision makers can still decrease false negatives and false positives by considering possible extraneous variables. Extraneous variables are those that account for the proportion of prediction that the universal screener does not. For example, teacher ratings, grades, assignment performance, and other factors may also be correlated with high-stakes testing performance and therefore may facilitate the prediction/identification process. Therefore, if other such variables are identified, there is nothing to preclude educational decision makers from conducting further diagnostic assessment to determine suitability for Tier II instruction.

False Positives

Another limitation of prediction is false positives. In this case, false positives are students who scored above the "meets expectations" cut score but failed to meet the cut score of 78 WRC per minute on the universal screening measure. False positives are a concern because they represent students who are identified as potentially needing more intensive and frequent educational instruction but who really do not. These types of errors result in schools allocating resources in an inefficient and ineffective manner. False positives can be minimized by attending to the same two considerations related to predictive validity and extraneous variables as explained in the discussion about false negatives.

Although it is difficult to correctly identify all students with a universal screening measure, it is possible to adequately identify a large proportion of the students who are at risk of not meeting expectations. By considering other variables that may account for the lack of a perfect prediction and ensuring the existence of a strong correlation between the universal screening measure and the high-stakes assessment, educators can identify students in an efficient, systematic, and accurate manner.

CONSIDERING RESOURCES WHEN ESTABLISHING CUT SCORES FOR USM-A

Although deriving cut scores through the use of statistical procedures such as correlations and even more sophisticated statistical procedures (such as logistic regression) are beyond the scope of this book (see Silberglitt, 2008), it is important to realize that a school can provide services only to the number of students that its resources will allow. Referring back to Figure 2.1, it should be apparent that although the school was able to clearly predict which students may have a lower probability of meeting expectations on a high-stakes assessment, it also was likely to falsely identify students. Using the proposed cut score alone, the school would be attempting to provide interventions to nearly half of the student population. This certainly is beyond the suggested benchmark of 80 percent of students meeting expectations. However, if the false positives are factored out, there would be no need to focus on the core curriculum as the area of needed change.

We have found that, after initial screening, it is often helpful to use a diagnostic tool to further factor out false positives. Diagnostic tools and use of those tools to make decisions are more fully discussed in Chapter 3. By using diagnostic tools after a screening process, educators and support personnel can more efficiently utilize resources by reducing the number of students (i.e., false positives) who may need Tier II services. In addition, diagnostic tools can also help focus Tier II intervention selection and development to maximize efficiency and effectiveness.

UNIVERSAL SCREENING MEASURES FOR SOCIAL BEHAVIOR (USM-B)

Social Behavior as an Important Component of RTI

Teaching social behavior to students is one of the most important priorities of educators. A student's ability to interact successfully, engage in schoolwork, make friends, and participate in other social aspects of schooling is predictive of a student's success not only in school but also after graduation. A student who develops a solid repertoire of social skills, has friends, and who is highly engaged and connected with his or her school and family is far less likely to develop antisocial behavior.

Although we see all learning as a behavior, clearly there are different domains of behavior that require different types of support. Because positive social behavior (like academic performance) is essential to student success, it is important to be systematic in the use of data-based decision making. In other words, as with academic skills, we need to monitor and make decisions about social behavior. Effective and efficient implementation of universal interventions that effect social behavior rests on three assumptions: (1) schools function as systems to support students with their behavior, (2) educators and other stakeholders who are part of the system need to analyze data based on the whole school's performance, and (3) someone needs to act on the data, using scientifically based intervention. Therefore, we need to screen, diagnose, and monitor progress with the purpose of data-based decision making in mind. This chapter focuses on social behavior screening and diagnosis; monitoring progress is addressed in subsequent chapters.

The most prevalent and practical approach to address social behavior outcomes that adheres to these three assumptions and uses an RTI framework is Positive Behavioral Interventions and Supports (PBIS; Sugai & Horner, 2002; Horner et al., 2009). Schoolwide PBIS has been defined as a model that emphasizes four integrated elements: (1) data-based decision making, (2) measurable outcomes, (3) effective behavior support practices with evidence that these outcomes are achievable, and (4) systems that efficiently and effectively support implementation of behavior (Sugai & Horner, 2002; Tobin & Sugai, 2005). The outcomes that have been observed through the implementation of the model range from less aversive/reactionary discipline practices (such as environments that are engaging, preventive, and productive for students) to a reduction in the number of office discipline referrals, tardiness, and antisocial behaviors (Horner et al., 2009).

Because of the effectiveness of this approach (and regardless of whether you are currently implementing PBIS in your school), most schools find that the principles related to PBIS as discussed throughout this book are useful in implementing a comprehensive model of RTI. In this section, we discuss how social behavior screening can be effectively and efficiently incorporated into a comprehensive model of RTI, similar to PBIS models. Likewise, we will discuss throughout the book how features of PBIS can be incorporated into a comprehensive RTI model.

Common Sense Is an Important Component to RTI

Before describing behavior screening in RTI, it is worth mentioning that dealing with students who have complex behaviors is a serious and multifaceted enterprise. And, although these decisions are best practice—and we encourage their use—we also encourage the use of sound educational judgment. This includes following district policies as well as state and federal laws and regulations.

Regardless of the approach outlined in this book or elsewhere, if a unique situation arises in which a student obviously needs support, please ensure that the student receives the supports or services he or she needs. There are acute crises that arise in the lives of children and adolescents that deserve immediate attention (e.g., suicide threat or attempt, bringing or threatening to bring a weapon to school, mental health hospitalization, juvenile justice contact, or death of primary caregiver). Apart from what they might score on an assessment or what tier they are at in an RTI process, students need immediate support in a crisis situation, and it is the responsibility of the administrative team and other educators in the school to make sure that children and adolescents receive the support they need.

SCREENING FOR STUDENTS AT RISK OF SOCIAL BEHAVIOR PROBLEMS

Office Discipline Referral Data: A Stand-Alone Externalizing Approach

One of the consistently demonstrated features in PBIS schools is the strong link between the universal screening measure of office discipline referrals (ODRs) and positive school climate. In addition to ODRs, many schools have found it useful to systematically track tardiness, absences, and other information about the referrals (such as where the problem behavior occurred and what triggered it).

Many schools have successfully used data obtained through systematic monitoring and analysis of ODRs and other variables to help identify students at risk of more intensive social behavior problems, which allows the schools to provide Tier II interventions to address such problems (Sugai, Sprague, Horner, & Walker, 2000; Tobin & Sugai, 1999). It has been suggested that anywhere from two to five ODRs during a single year is a good criterion for identifying students for Tier II behavior interventions (Sugai et al., 2000).

Office discipline referrals are often divided into major and minor offenses in order to separate small, common problems a teacher may deal with from more serious problems such as a student hitting a classmate. Figure 2.5 is a sample office discipline referral form. A copy of this form is also available in the appendix and on the accompanying CD. This form can be easily tailored to fit the unique problem behaviors of any school. Some schools also create categories to better help them understand social behavior problems. Behaviors can be categorized as internalizing (e.g., withdrawn, excessively shy) or externalizing (e.g., aggression, arguing).

Major ODRs are the most commonly used indicators of negative social behavior. However, some schools like to consider minor ODRs as well. Although there is no clear guideline, it is worth noting that minor infractions can be an indicator of a low-level chronic behavior problem that might be easily remediated with a Tier II social behavior intervention. Some schools, however, choose not to issue minor ODRs because they feel it leads to over-reporting of problems that the teacher should attempt to deal with by implementing effective classroom management practices. We have found no current research on the issue of tracking and using minor referrals for the purposes of screening, but we encourage schools to use what "fits best" for the students they serve and for the school's unique instructional circumstances. Finally, any decisions on what to track or not should always be driven by the best empirical evidence and data available.

FIGURE 2.5   Example of an ODR form.

OFFICE DISCIPLINE REFERRAL FORM

Student: _____ Grade: _____ Referring Staff: _____

Date of Referral: _____ Time of Behavior: _____

LOCATION	EXTERNALIZING BEHAVIOR	INTERNALIZING BEHAVIOR
☐ Classroom #____ ☐ Hallway ☐ Cafeteria ☐ Library ☐ Bathroom _____ ☐ Bus ☐ Open yard ☐ In front of school ☐ Parking lot ☐ Other (please specify): _____ _____	☐ Abusive language ☐ Physical contact ☐ Sexual language toward peer or adult ☐ Lying ☐ Cheating ☐ Vandalism ☐ Smoking ☐ Truant from class ☐ Other (please specify): _____ _____	*For internalizing referrals, send form to office with a description of the problem, but do not send student to the office unless necessary.* ☐ Does not talk with peers ☐ Excessively shy/withdrawn ☐ Avoids social interaction ☐ Appears fearful in nonthreatening situations ☐ Fails to assert self ☐ Unresponsive to social situations ☐ Does not participate in social activities ☐ Other (please specify): _____ _____
ANTECEDENT	BEHAVIOR	CONSEQUENCE

Comments:

_____

_____

_____

_____

_____

_____

_____

_____

Although tracking ODRs has been validated as a whole-school indicator of school climate (Irvin, Tobin, Sprague, Sugai, & Vincent, 2004), some problems have been found when attempting to use ODR tracking to detect more-nuanced behaviors such as internalizing behavior problems (withdrawal, verbalizing body pains that have no medical origin, etc.) that are often related to severity levels indicative of depression, anxiety, or other potential psychiatric diagnoses. Some researchers (e.g., Walker, Cheney, Stage, Blum, & Horner, 2005) have found that screening combined with ODR tracking may be a very useful and practical resolution for addressing this problem.

Screening for Externalizing and Internalizing Problems

For a number of reasons, the Systematic Screening for Behavior Disorders (SSBD) (Walker & Severson, 1991) is viewed by educators and researchers as the gold standard for effective and efficient screening for externalizing and internalizing problems. First, it is easy to train people to use. Second, it requires less time to complete than many other systems (such as the Behavior Assessment System for Children, BASC; Kamphaus & Reynolds, 2009). The multi-step process that we discuss draws heavily from that of the SSBD.

Figure 2.6 outlines the general model for identifying students at risk of serious behavior problems that would require some level of intervention. Although we advocate for a multi-step process, we focus only on the first step (teacher nomination and ODRs) in this chapter because it is the initial screening step in the identification process. The other steps (follow-up confirmation, functional assessment, and functional analysis) are addressed in Chapter 3.

Initial Screening

Consistent with SSBD (Walker & Severson, 1991), the initial step of most screening protocols is to have teachers categorize students in their classrooms as having externalizing or

FIGURE 2.6   **Framework for assessing social behavior from universal screening to individual diagnostic assessment.**

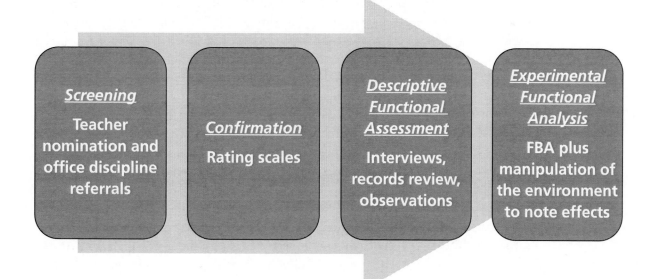

internalizing problems (at the secondary education level, one teacher can complete the screening or several teachers can work in teams). As part of the categorization process, students are identified as either internalizers or externalizers (see Figure 2.7 for an example of a ranking sheet). Typically, students are placed in one column or the other and then ranked in order of how strongly they demonstrate the internalizing or externalizing behaviors. Although student behavior is often more complex than the ranking sheet shows, making the choice facilitates an accurate screening process. So, teachers should pick which best describes each student. Sometimes, educators have a hard time deciding on the rank of particular students. It is important to trust one's instincts as an educator and simply make a decision. There will be opportunities for more thorough follow-up, if needed to confirm the ranking decision. Research suggests that educators can make good decisions through this categorizing and ranking process (Walker et al., 1994).

When identifying students as internalizers or externalizers, it is important to wait one month after school starts before starting the screening process because it takes time for children and adolescents to adjust to the new school year, and educators need at least one month to get to know their students before they can make informed decisions about them. Once the screening is performed, the top three students in each column are considered at risk for significant behavior problems, and diagnostic procedures can begin (see Chapter 3).

DATA-BASED DECISION MAKING USING UNIVERSAL SCREENING MEASURES FOR SOCIAL BEHAVIOR

Computer-Based Analysis for Social Behavior

Although teachers may nominate students that they suspect as being at risk, ODR data are collected as the infractions occur. Data are collected using an ODR form and must be tabulated and analyzed. Many schools track, tabulate, and analyze these data using computer or Web-based programs. Although there are many programs available, we suggest that educators shop around for the one that best suits their needs and is the most cost effective. There are many programs for managing data, such as the School-Wide Information System (SWIS™; May et al., 2008). SWIS is a Web-based program commonly used to track office discipline referrals in schools implementing PBIS. Although these programs are useful and functional, for the purpose of discussion we provide an overview of data-based decision making for social behavior across the tiers using simple charts constructed in Microsoft Excel. It is an effective way to screen for students at risk of more significant problem behavior and monitor their progress in a comprehensive RTI model.

Data obtained from ODRs can be disaggregated over time so that the entire school year can be analyzed on a monthly basis (shown as Figure 2.8). The figure shows that few students are receiving office discipline referrals. Schools that have students with more office referrals may need more resources to support secondary or tertiary prevention.

In addition, data can also be graphed depicting the problem behavior (Figure 2.9), location (Figure 2.10), time of day (Figure 2.11), and student (Figure 2.12). An advantage of these graphs is that they can be generated throughout the year or at key times. We recommend that problem-solving teams check these data at least monthly—preferably twice a month. Administrators who receive ODR information should be comfortable using and

FIGURE 2.7   Example of a ranking sheet of internalizers and externalizers.

	Externalizing		Internalizing
1	Mark Stevens	1	Debbie Roberts
2	Gary Palms	2	Emily Fredricks
3	Craig Hatt	3	Mark Stevens
4	Dellia Jones	4	James Rinaldi
5	Andy Redson	5	Red Carlson
6	Stefine Aniter	6	Conner Dells
7	Gavin Paulson	7	Hunter Rains
8	Jeff Blankinship	8	Janet Acers
9	Juan Garcia	9	Soozie Fulk
10	Jerry Franks	10	Melissa Stevens

FIGURE 2.8   Example of schoolwide data analyzed per month.

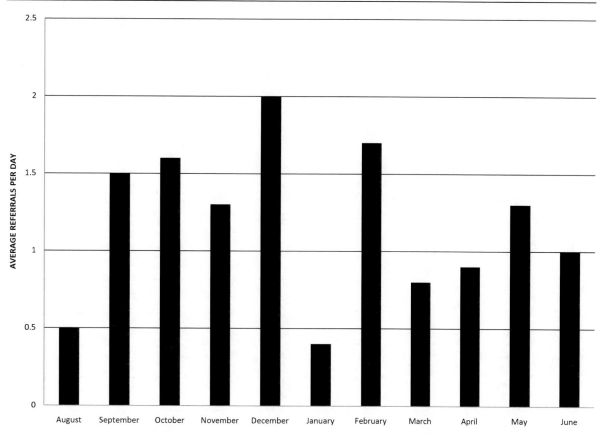

checking data frequently to make sure that students are appropriately identified between problem-solving team meetings.

Once such data are available, educators can use them to make decisions on how to allocate resources and focus instruction. For example, a school might find, as shown in Figure 2.10, that a high percentage of their office referrals occur from events taking place in hallways. Although most of the referrals stem from behavior in the classroom, and that

FIGURE 2.9   Example of schoolwide data analyzed by problem behavior.

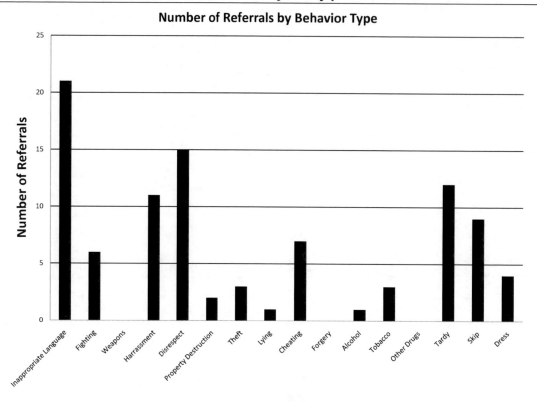

Number of Referrals by Behavior Type

FIGURE 2.10   Example of schoolwide data analyzed by location.

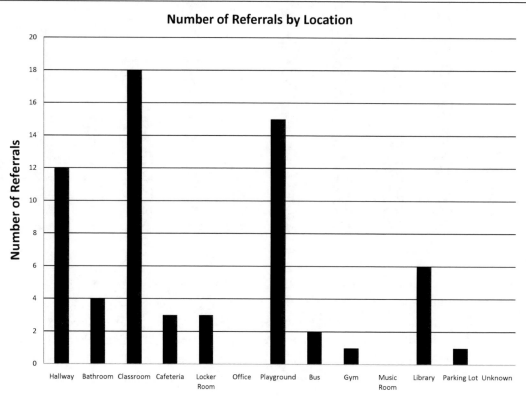

Number of Referrals by Location

FIGURE 2.11   Example of schoolwide data analyzed by time of day.

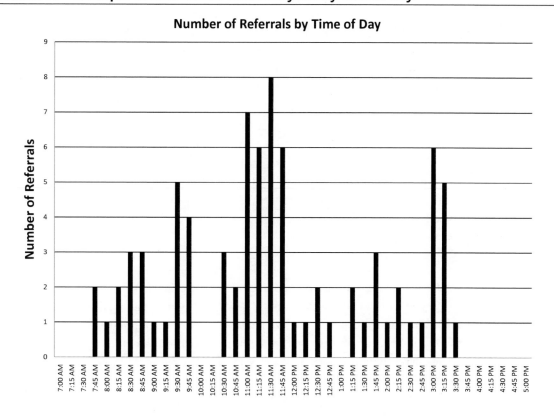

Number of Referrals by Time of Day

FIGURE 2.12   Example of schoolwide data analyzed by student.

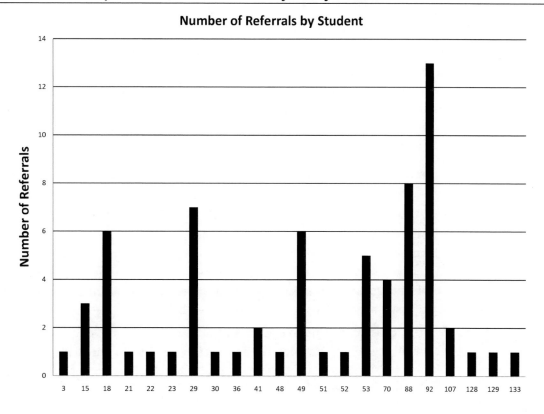

Number of Referrals by Student

is always a concern, it does not represent an unusual pattern for schools. However, the frequency of referrals from infractions occurring in hallways is especially notable and may need to be addressed. The team may, for example, decide that they need to re-teach expectations about hallway behavior in the core curriculum.

Although this type of global information is useful, problem-solving teams may want to analyze data further to see why students are being referred. Specific problems such as fighting might be addressed differently than behaviors such as yelling and being disruptive. When analyzing whole-school data, teams should attempt to identify what triggers students to behave in such a way that warrants referrals. The triggers are not always easy to identify, but by using data and the problem-solving process (discussed in Chapter 5), teams can often find creative solutions to reduce the number of office referrals in a particular category. Likewise, it is important that the effectiveness of any solutions that are implemented be analyzed.

A Behavior–Academic Link

It is our experience that schools can be much more efficient if the problem-solving team addresses data on social behavior and academic performance together. It is quite possible that academic issues can be connected to behavior problems and to the ability of students to be engaged in academic work. If students are consistently sent to the office as a method of resolving behavior problems in the classroom, it is likely an indicator of a negative school climate, and it may be interfering with academic learning (i.e., students are missing instruction). When data-based decision making is coordinated in this fashion, it helps a school improve behavior *and* academic outcomes.

SUMMARY OF IMPORTANT POINTS

This chapter provided a foundation for understanding universal screening measures. After reading this chapter, you are encouraged to read Chapter 7. That chapter addresses important considerations and lessons learned, which you are likely to find helpful in understanding and navigating the challenges that come with the implementation of universal screening measures (such as scoring, reporting results, and training personnel). The following important points about universal screening measures should be shared with any staff you may be working with in the early stages of implementation.

□ **Universal screening measures are used for screening and for monitoring progress.** Universal screening measures are not diagnostic tools; they are used to screen for potential problems and sometimes for monitoring student progress over time.

□ **There are five characteristics of universal screening measures.** (1) They are brief to administer, (2) they allow for repeated measurement of student performance each year, (3) they are simple to score and interpret, (4) they reduce the number of students needing diagnostic assessment, and (5) they predict academic performance on high-stakes tests and can help identify more serious behavioral concerns.

□ **USM-A focus on the "big five" skills in reading.** Screening tools in reading focus on phonemic awareness, phonics, fluency, vocabulary, and comprehension. Currently, fluency measures seem to be the most robust tools. Although comprehension and vocabulary screening tools are being developed, they are less predictive of high-stakes testing performance. Reading assessments are generally administered to students individually, with the exception of a few lesser predictive measures such as Maze, Cloze, and True–False, which are administered to a group.

◻ **USM-A focus on math calculation and applied problems in mathematics.** Assessment tools are being developed, and research suggests that they show promise. Tools are available both commercially and free of charge. These tools are generally administered in a classwide format.

◻ **USM-A focus on correct letter and word sequences for spelling and writing.** Similar to USM-A in reading and math, written expression (writing and spelling) is assessed using sensitive measures. These tools are generally administered in a classwide format.

◻ **There are many ways to set cut scores for USM-A.** Although there are many ways to utilize data from USM-A, such as percentile ranks, dual discrepancy, and the standards-based approach, it is important to consider the resources available to the school when identifying students in need of additional services. To allocate resources effectively, cut scores, or benchmarks, can be used to select students to receive support and intervention services.

◻ **Social behavior is an important component of RTI.** Just as important as screening for academic concerns is universal screening for behavior (USM-B).

◻ **Common sense is also an important component of RTI.** If a student exhibits behavior that warrants immediate attention (e.g., the student is a danger to himself or herself or to others), then the entire screening and confirmation steps of the process should be bypassed in order to protect the individuals involved.

◻ **Office discipline referrals are an important variable to analyze.** This is particularly true at the whole-school level where it is possible—and useful—to track ODRs by time, location, student, and so forth. In addition, ODR analysis also helps in identifying specific students who might need intervention and support services. ODRs are particularly important to the screening process.

◻ **Internalizing behaviors should be screened for, too.** Internalized negative behaviors are just as important to identify as externalized ones, and it is not uncommon for students who exhibit internalizing behaviors to be overlooked when identifying those in need of Tier II services. It is suggested that an empirically supported process similar to the SSBD be conducted to guard against this possibility.

◻ **Confirmation is more complex than screening.** Confirmation requires administration of additional assessment tools, while screening simply requires only a categorization and ranking process of internalizers and externalizers by teachers and an analysis of ODR. The confirmation assessments are required, however, because they are important in weeding out false positives and false negatives.

◻ **Using technology to make data-based decisions related to USM-B is helpful.** Programs such as SWIS can be very helpful in grouping data for analysis. Many types of programs are available. It is important that the data analyzers choose a program that best suits their needs and budget.

◻ **Remember, there is a behavior–academic link.** Academic problems are sometimes a precursor to behavior problems, and vice versa. It is important to address both of these areas when a problem in one area is initially identified.

REFERENCES

Deno, S. L. (1989). Curriculum-based measurement and special education services. A fundamental and direct relationship. In M. Shinn (Ed.), *Curriculum-based measurement: Assessing special children*. New York, NY: Guilford.

Fuchs, L. S., Fuchs, D., Hosp, M. K., & Jenkins, J. R. (2001). Oral reading fluency as an indicator of reading competence: A theoretical, empirical, and historical analysis. *Scientific Studies of Reading, 5,* 239–256.

Horner, R. H., Sugai, G., Smolkowski, K., Eber, L., Nakasato, J., Todd, A. W., & Esperanza, J. (2009). A randomized, wait-list controlled effectiveness trial assessing school-wide positive behavior support in elementary schools. *Journal of Positive Behavior Interventions, 11*(3), 133–144.

Irvin, L.K., Tobin, T. J., Sprague, J. R., Sugai, G., & Vincent, C. G. (2004). Validity of office discipline referral measures as indices of school-wide behavioral status and effects of school-wide behavioral interventions. *Journal of Positive Behavior Interventions, 6,* 131–147.

Kamphaus, R. W., & Reynolds, C. (2009). BASC™-2 *Behavior Assessment System for Children* (2nd ed.). San Antonio, TX: Pearson Education.

May, S., Ard, W., Todd, A., Horner, R., Glasgow, A., Sugai, G., & Sprague, J. (2008). *School-wide Information System*. Eugene, OR: University of Oregon, Educational and Community Supports.

National Institute of Child Health and Human Development. (2000). Report of the National Reading Panel. *Teaching children to read: An evidence-based assessment of the scientific research literature on reading and its implications for reading instruction*. www.nichd.nih.gov/publications/nrp/smallbook.htm

No Child Left Behind Act, Pub. L. No. 107–110 (2001).

Silberglitt, B. (2008). Best practices in using technology for data-based decision making. In A. Thomas and J. Grimes, (Eds.), *Best practices in school psychology V.* Bethesda, MD: National Association of School Psychologists.

Sugai, G., & Horner, R. (2002). The evolution of discipline practices: School-wide positive behavior supports. *Child and Family Behavior Therapy, 24,* 23–50.

Sugai, G., Sprague, J. Horner, R., & Walker, H. (2000). Preventing school violence: The use of office referral to assess and monitor school-wide discipline interventions. *Journal of Emotional and Behavioral Disorders, 8*(2), 94–101.

Tobin, T. J., & Sugai, G. (1999). Using sixth-grade school records to predict violence, chronic discipline problems, and high school outcomes. *Journal of Emotional and Behavioral Disorders, 7,* 40–53.

Tobin, T. J., & Sugai, G. (2005). Preventing problem behaviors: Primary, secondary, and tertiary level prevention interventions for young children. *Journal of Early Intensive Behavior Intervention, 2*(3), 115–124.

Walker, B., Cheney, D., Stage, S., Blum, C., & Horner, R. H. (2005). Schoolwide screening and positive behavior supports: Identifying and supporting students at risk for school failure. *Journal of Positive Behavior Interventions, 7*(4), 194–204.

Walker, H., & Severson, H. H. (1991). *Systematic screening for behavior disorders.* Longmont, CO: Sopris West.

Walker, H. M., Severson, H., Nicholson F., Kehle, T., Jenson, W., & Clark, E. (1994). Replication of the Systematic Screening for Behavior Disorders (SSBD) procedure for the identification of at-risk children. *Journal of Emotional and Behavior Disorders, 2,* 66–77.

RECOMMENDED RESOURCES

AIMSweb

www.aimsweb.com

DIBELS Data System

http://dibels.uoregon.edu

easyCBM

http://easycbm.com

Positive Behavioral Interventions and Supports

www.pbis.org

School-Wide Information System

www.swis.org

Diagnostic Tools and Procedures for Assessing Academic Performance and Social Behavior

CHAPTER OVERVIEW

Diagnostic tools and procedures are essential to maximizing efficiency and effectiveness of the RTI process. This chapter aids in the understanding of diagnostic procedures for both academic performance and social behavior. The chapter seeks to build on the previous chapters' objectives. Specifically this chapter will:

- □ Provide a purpose, rationale, and description of what constitutes a diagnostic tool for academic performance and social behavior.

- □ Provide examples of diagnostic tools for academic performance and social behavior.

- □ Outline how diagnostic tools may differ across Tiers II and III.

- □ Describe how to make data-based decisions related to diagnostic tools for academic performance and social behavior.

- □ Describe the commonalities and differences between diagnostic tools for academic performance and diagnostic tools for social behavior.

PURPOSES OF DIAGNOSTIC TOOLS

A diagnostic tool (DT) may be used to (1) follow up with any student identified on the USM as potentially needing additional support, (2) identify a specific skill or subset of skills for which students might need additional instructional support, and (3) assist in linking students with skills deficits to empirically supported intervention. Diagnostic tools and procedures should be utilized for reading, mathematics, written expression, and social behavior.

RATIONALE FOR DIAGNOSTIC TOOLS

Continuing with the medical analogy of the previous chapter, DTs for academic performance or social behavior are similar to tools used for making medical diagnoses. After screening for general health, a medical practitioner may find that blood pressure is high and conclude that further tests are needed, such as a blood test and/or an electrocardiogram. The idea is to (1) rule out any previous concerns flagged by a screening procedure, (2) find an appropriate diagnosis, and/or (3) identify an effective treatment. With regard to RTI, after an appropriate diagnosis is made using a diagnostic tool, an effective academic or social behavior intervention can be identified.

CHARACTERISTICS OF DIAGNOSTIC TOOLS

Given this rationale, there are a few general characteristics inherent to diagnostic tools for academic performance and social behavior. First, a DT is likely (but not always) to be administered in a one-to-one format. It is important to point out, however, that some DT administrations are made via computer. Second, a DT requires more time to administer than a USM. Because a purpose of the DT is to pinpoint the specific place to start intervention, it requires more than just a couple of minutes. Finally, a DT will generally have a wider variety of items than a USM. A USM provides only a snapshot of a single characteristic that is likely to be predictive of more specific problems, but a DT is required to determine what characteristic(s) may need to be targeted specifically.

For example, a physician does not target weight specifically, because it is only an *indicator* of unhealthy behavior. She is likely to target *specific* behaviors, such as overeating and lack of exercise. Likewise, an educator may find that the number of correct sentences written is a positive quality indicator. However, instead of attempting to target the number of sentences a student writes, the educator may need to focus on capitalization, punctuation, grammar, organization of writing, and other criteria. A DT for writing would require more time to administer and score, but it would allow sufficient sampling of a variety of writing items to facilitate an accurate diagnosis of writing skills deficit(s) and thus allow for better prescription of an intervention known to target those areas. The DT allows an educator to move from simply measuring an indicator of educational health toward a more specific diagnosis of a particular skill deficiency or deficiencies.

SELECTION OF DIAGNOSTIC TOOLS

The type of DT selected for a given area may depend on the level of support (i.e., tier) required. For example, if, after screening, a student is identified as potentially needing Tier II support, a diagnostic tool for academic performance (DT-A) is administered to identify the potential skill areas in need of remediation. However, a student who has already received Tier II intervention services may need more-intensive individualized intervention if he or she is not demonstrating adequate progress. Just as the level of intensity of the intervention is likely to increase, so is the level of diagnostic assessment. Although a DT for Tier II may be provided to anyone who did not meet a benchmark on the screening measures, the DT for Tier III may be more individually tailored and more "experimental" in approach. Moreover, the administration of such DTs generally requires substantially more training and expertise. This is true of DTs for both academic performance and social behavior.

DIAGNOSTIC TOOLS FOR ACADEMIC PERFORMANCE (DT-A)

DT-A for Tier I

Sometimes it is apparent that Tier I instruction should be the focus of improvement. This determination is often made when a particular level of analysis (i.e., schoolwide, grade level, or teacher administered) is not conforming to the proposed model (e.g., 80 percent of students meeting benchmark expectations or making AYP). It is apparent that an analysis of the problem is warranted. One method for analyzing Tier I instruction is to utilize an instructional analysis form (IAF). An example of an IAF is provided in Figure 3.1 (a reproducible form is available in the appendix and on the CD that comes with this book). Note that in first grade, one might expect that more time should be spent in phonic instruction and less in short-interval, group-based reading with limited accountability. Moreover, it is likely also more important to focus on active, overt student responses to a larger degree than to infer student responses during activities in which individual accountability is limited (such as silent reading or choral reading).

DT-A for Tier II (Standard Protocol Assessment)

After a student is identified by a universal screening measure for academic performance (USM-A) as potentially being at risk of not meeting high-stakes testing assessment expectations, it is important to follow up with a more informative assessment in hope of identifying the general area or areas to be targeted. For example, two different students not meeting cut-score levels on the USM-A for reading does not necessarily mean that they require the same intervention. It is quite possible that one student requires a vocabulary-building intervention while the other requires a phonics-building intervention. A primary function of the DT-A is to facilitate this intervention linking process. Table 3.1 provides examples of diagnostic tools commonly used to assess various academic subjects. (It also provides examples of DTs for assessing social behavior, as described more fully in the next section.)

After a DT-A for Tier II is conducted, students who do not meet a given expectation or benchmark are provided a standard protocol intervention. If it is determined that the student does meet acceptable benchmarks or expectations on the DT-A for Tier II, then a team decision based on other data and a consideration of available resources is made with regard to whether the student receives the Tier II level of support. It is important that multiple data sources be considered in determining whether a student should or should not receive the services and that the DT-A be only one of these data sources. Moreover, the DT-A should facilitate identification of the appropriate focus of the standard protocol intervention to be provided.

DT-A for Tier III (Individualized Hypothesis Testing)

A student who does not demonstrate adequate progress toward the school's standard protocol may require more-intensive intervention. The question becomes "What intervention does

FIGURE 3.1   **Example of an instructional analysis form for first grade.**

Instructional Analysis Form

Skill	Teaching Strategy	Materials	Format	Allocated Time	Reward or Reinforcer	Method of Assessment
Reading Fluency	Choral Reading	Reading from Books	Classwide	5 minutes	Praise	Listening to student
Reading Accuracy	Word Wall Words	Words on Wall	Classwide	10 minutes	Praise	Listening to three students at a time
Comprehension	Reading Story to Student	Chapter Book	Front of Class	10 minutes	Free drawing at the same time	Asking direct questions and seeing who volunteers
Letter Naming	Drilling	Flash Cards	Around the World	10 minutes	Competition	None

this student need in addition to what is already provided?" To answer this question, you will have to provide more-individualized assessment, develop a hypothesis, and then implement an intervention designed to test the hypothesis. This type of process is commonly referred to as curriculum-based evaluation (CBE; Howell & Nolet, 2000).

Consider the following example. A fourth-grade student, Tammy, scored below the benchmark in the fall and subsequently was provided with a Tier II standard assessment protocol. It was determined that her performance on the DT-A for Tier II was also low, and she was therefore provided with a Tier II standard protocol intervention that focused on building basic math facts. Despite her progress in improved fluency of the basic facts of addition, subtraction, multiplication, and division, she was still not meeting the benchmark in the winter. Moreover, her math grade had also decreased. It was decided that Tammy would benefit from an individualized DT-A in math. The school psychologist created an individualized DT for Tammy using a probe generator (Wright, 2010). The psychologist determined that Tammy was fluent with the basic facts and considered assessing the next level of math (two-digit addition, subtraction, multiplication, and division with and without regrouping).

Figure 3.2 displays an academic skills assessment of basic operations for Tammy. Tammy was able to successfully complete various types of problems. However, a pattern emerges in Tammy's performance. Specifically, she appeared to respond inaccurately or skip problems that required regrouping during subtraction. It is interesting to note that she was able to complete multiplication problems and basic division facts accurately. This type of analysis prompted the school psychologist to hypothesize that Tammy needs additional instruction focusing on subtraction problems that require regrouping. Because the Tier II intervention focused on fluency building of basic facts, it did not fully target Tammy's instructional needs. The data analysis showed that Tammy should be provided

TABLE 3.1 Commonly used diagnostic tools.

Test	Domain	Administration Time	Ages/Grade	Format	Additional Information
KeyMath3™	Math	45–90 minutes	Grades K–12	One to one	http://tinyurl.com/keymath3
Fountas & Pinnell	Reading	30–45 minutes	Grades K–8	One to one, paper-based	http://www.heinemann.com/fountasandpinnell
Measures of Academic Progress	Reading Math Language Usage Science	20–45 minutes	Grades K–8	Computer	http://tinyurl.com/measures-of-academic-progress
Systematic Screening for Behavior Disorders	Behavior	10 minutes for checklist; 15 minutes for observation	Grades K–6	Paper-based checklist, classroom observation	http://tinyurl.com/ss-behavior-disorders
Behavioral & Emotional Screening System	Behavior	5–20 minutes	Grades Preschool–12	Paper-based; computer scoring available	Parent, teacher, and self-report versions available. http://tinyurl.com/basc-2-system
Developmental Reading Assessment, 2nd Edition	Reading	Varies depending on level; ranges 15–40 minutes	Grades K–8; K–6 (Spanish version)	Paper-based or digital	Spanish version also available. http://www.pearsonschool.com
Child Behavior Checklist	Behavior	15–60 minutes	Ages 6–18	Paper-based; computer scoring available	Parent and teacher versions available. http://tinyurl.com/cbcl6-18
Illinois Snapshots of Early Literacy	Reading	20 minutes	Grades K–2	Classroom-based	Spanish version also available. http://www.isbe.state.il.us/curriculum/reading/html/isel.htm

(continued)

Table 3.1 (continued)

Test	Domain	Administration Time	Ages/Grade	Format	Additional Information
Tungsten Learning's Benchmark Assessment System	Reading Math Science Social Studies	40 minutes	Grades 2–8	Computer-based	http://tinyurl.com/tungsten-bas
Rigby Reads (Reading Evaluation & Diagnostic System)	Reading	Varies depending on level and skills assessed	Grades K–3	Paper-based	http://tinyurl.com/rigby-reads
Running Records	Reading			One to one	http://www.readinga-z.com/guided/runrecord.html
Woodcock Reading Master Test	Reading	10–30 minutes per cluster	Grades K–12	One to one	http://tinyurl.com/woodcock-rmt
Informal Reading Inventory, 6th ed.	Reading	10 minutes	Grades K–12	One to one	Burns, P.C, & Roe, B.D. (2002). Orlando, FL: Houghton Mifflin Harcourt
Test of Written Language	Writing	60–90 minutes	Ages 9–17	One to one	http://tinyurl.com/test-of-written-language
Jerry Johns Basic Reading Inventory	Reading	30–60 minutes	K–12	One to one	http://tinyurl.com/jerryjohns-bri
Oral Written Language Scales	Oral and Written Language	30–80 minutes	Ages 3–21	One to one	http://tinyurl.com/oral-wls
Test of Written Spelling	Written Spelling	Within 20 minutes	Grades 1–12	One to one	http://tinyurl.com/test-of-written-spelling

FIGURE 3.2   **Example of an error analysis for math computation.**

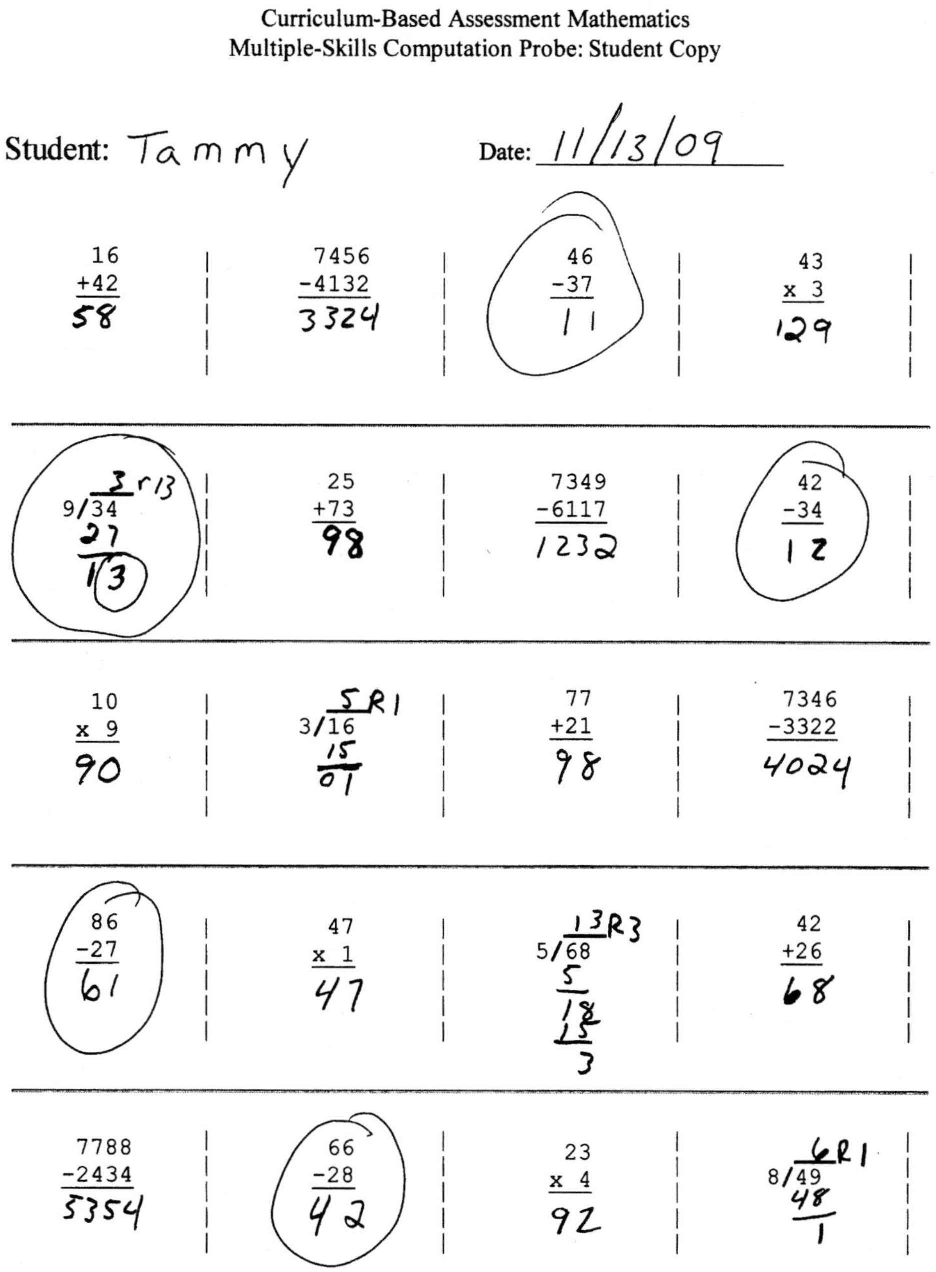

Curriculum-Based Assessment Mathematics
Multiple-Skills Computation Probe: Student Copy

Student: Tammy   Date: 11/13/09

16 +42 **58**	7456 −4132 **3324**	*(46 −37 **11**)*	43 x 3 **129**

*(3 r13 9/34 27 **13**)*	25 +73 **98**	7349 −6117 **1232**	*(42 −34 **12**)*

10 x 9 **90**	5 R1 3/16 15 0	77 +21 **98**	7346 −3322 **4024**

*(86 −27 **61**)*	47 x 1 **47**	13 R3 5/68 5 18 15 3	42 +26 **68**

7788 −2434 **5354**	*(66 −28 **42**)*	23 x 4 **92**	6 R1 8/49 48 1

with individualized support in this more specific skill while continuing to have her progress monitored.

This method of CBE and hypothesis development methodology is critical for identifying individualized instructional needs. Although the example focused on math, similar methodology may be applied to all other academic areas. In reading, for example, it is likely that students who read quickly but inaccurately require different interventions (error correction interventions) than students who read accurately but slowly (fluency interventions). Moreover, two students who read inaccurately may respond differently to various error correction procedures. A student who makes many substitution errors may require some training in discriminating between the target word to be read and the word that was actually said, while a student who pauses at words he or she does not know may require prompting or modeling. Reading comprehension may focus on the extent to which students utilize comprehension strategies (such as previewing questions/text, self-reflection, and prediction). Writing may focus on error patterns dealing with punctuation, grammar, capitalization, syntax, vocabulary, style, paragraph structure, and other skills. By providing students with opportunities to respond to academic tasks and then analyzing the tasks for specific error patterns (i.e., inappropriate behavior), school personnel may be better equipped to link assessment data with intervention procedures aimed at improving performance.

It should be pointed out that an individualized DT-A may often be similar to a USM or standard follow-up DT-A for Tier II. The difference is that the USM-A or standard follow-up DT-A for Tier II is extended to include a larger variety and number of responses such that an error analysis of specific skills can be conducted. Another point to be made is that not every individualized DT needs to be constructed by school personnel. An individualized DT-A could include commercial instruments that provide a sufficient sampling of the academic domain with regard to number and type of items to allow for adequate error analysis. For example, KeyMath3™ (Connoly, 2008) may provide a sufficient number and array of problems to allow hypotheses to be developed related to understanding student responses—specifically, the "weaknesses" in specific skill areas. These hypotheses can then be tested by linking them to interventions aimed at facilitating accurate and efficient response to the specific skill-area deficits identified.

DIAGNOSTIC TOOLS FOR SOCIAL BEHAVIOR (DT-B)

DT-B Tier II (Standard Protocol Assessment)

After preliminary identification of students through rapid screening measures such as office discipline referrals and teacher nominations (as discussed in Chapter 2), it is important to follow up the screening, for two reasons. First, school personnel want to confirm the students identified by the USM—having too many students falsely identified (false positives) as needing Tier II intervention can overtax the RTI system. Second, school personnel want to link students to an appropriate intervention. Providing a student with a group intervention that focuses on externalizing problem behaviors when the student actually needs intervention focusing on internalizing issues may be counterproductive. Following up the USM-B with a DT-B helps limit the number of students falsely identified and better links students to an appropriate standard protocol intervention. Table 3.1 lists some diagnostic tools commonly used for social behavior assessment.

Although there are many DT-Bs, we focus our discussion on Systematic Screening for Behavior Disorders (SSBD; Walker and Severson, 1991) as a general framework, as we did in Chapter 2. In Chapter 2, we focused on screening (teacher nominations and ODRs). In this chapter, we focus on confirmation of teacher nominations and ODR screening in identifying students as being at risk and in need of additional behavioral intervention.

Educators often have accurate impressions of students' social and behavioral challenges, but those impressions need to be confirmed. In addition, educators often focus on students who have externalizing problem behaviors—the students who are most disruptive to the learning environment—and may overlook students who exhibit internalizing problems. Having a process that first requires teachers to nominate students who demonstrate either internalizing or externalizing behaviors—then confirming that those nominations are accurate through use of an empirically validated rating scale or set of rating scales—is essential to pinpointing groups of students for systematic Tier II intervention.

Teacher nominations are confirmed by the administration of follow-up assessment instruments (i.e., rating scales) to the top three internalizing and top three externalizing students. Those follow-up assessment instruments on the SSBD are the Critical Events Inventory, the Adaptive Scale, and the Maladaptive Scale. The Critical Events Inventory is a list of 33 items, such as setting fires, physically assaulting an adult, stealing, being sexually abused, or sexually abusing others. These crisis events can possibly be indicative of more serious behavior problems in the future. Although there are 33 critical events listed on the Critical Events Inventory, it also includes a place to identify events that may qualify as critical that might not already be listed. The Adaptive Scale screens for the presence of basic adaptive social skills in school environments (e.g., following teacher directions, cooperating with peers). The Maladaptive Scale screens for students at risk for developing antisocial behaviors (e.g., manipulating other children, testing teacher limits).

It should be pointed out that the Critical Events Inventory is unique to the SSBD. A second point to be made is that schools that do not utilize the SSBD use other, broader-based measures to screen for externalizing and/or internalizing problems, such as the Behavior Assessment System for Children (BASC; Kamphaus & Reynolds, 2009) or the Achenbach System of Empirically Based Assessment (ASEBA; Achenbach, 2010). Figure 3.3 displays a suggested outline of the assessment process for behavior disorders in a comprehensive RTI model.

One step worthy of special mention is the analysis of the subscale scores. Typically, a student is said to need intervention only when he or she meets specified criteria on the follow-up rating scales or on the Maladaptive and/or Adaptive Scales on the SSBD. We believe that in a comprehensive RTI school there are many data sources that should be considered in addition to these subscales at this point—that is, if a student does not meet criteria on the follow-up rating scales, he or she may still require intervention if other known data suggest the behavior is of a sufficiently severe level. Some questions to consider in making this decision may include the following:

◻ Does the student have two or more office referrals, a suspension, excessive tardiness, and/or absences that might be related to the behavior challenges?

◻ Are there other indications that the student has poor social skills (e.g., few or no friends, infrequent or poor-quality interactions with peers or staff)?

Although there are no definitive criteria for these types of data, teams should discuss them in context of the SSBD data. If there is a chance that the student might benefit from Tier II interventions and school resources can support it, then the provision of support is warranted. Then, if no change is observed over a period of 4 to 6 weeks, the direct observation protocol for the descriptive functional assessment can be implemented.

DT-B for Tier III (Individualized Hypothesis Testing)

As with the DT-A for Tier III described in a previous section of this chapter, a student who does not demonstrate adequate progress toward the school's standard protocol for behavior

FIGURE 3.3   **General process for identification and confirmation of students at risk for internalizing and/or externalizing problems.**

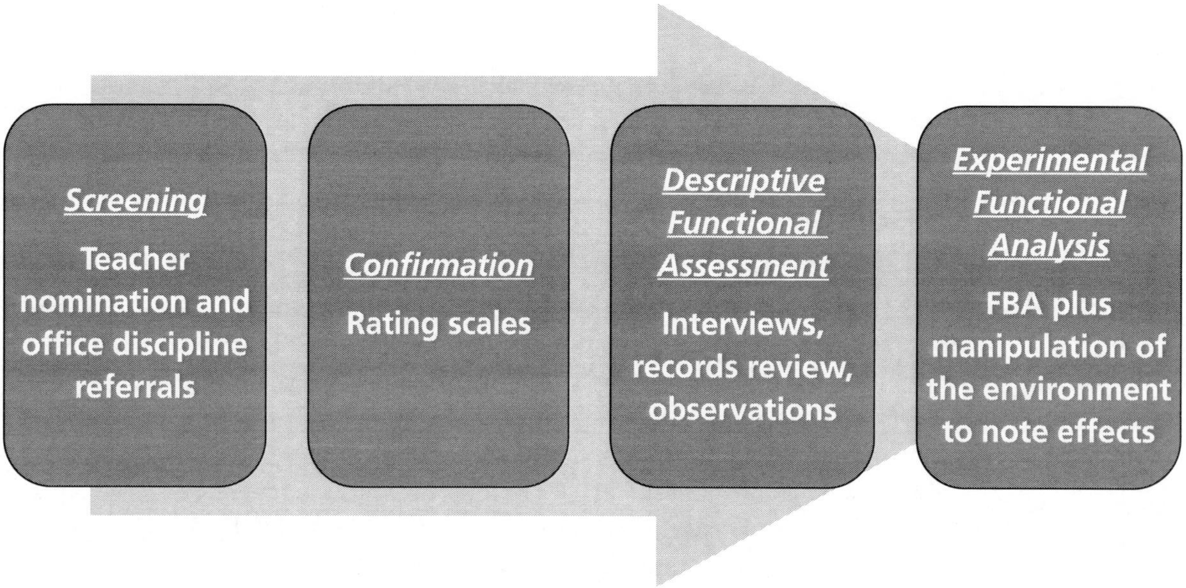

Screening

Teacher nomination and office discipline referrals

Confirmation

Rating scales

Descriptive Functional Assessment

Interviews, records review, observations

Experimental Functional Analysis

FBA plus manipulation of the environment to note effects

may require more-intensive intervention. To determine the additional intervention(s) needed for that student, you will have to provide more-intensive individualized assessment, develop a hypothesis, and then implement an intervention designed to test the hypothesis. This process, when applied to social behavior, is commonly referred to as functional behavior assessment (FBA; Steege & Watson, 2009). Functional behavior assessment is a process of identifying the variables that trigger or serve as a function of a behavior of interest. It is important to point out that an FBA has three important basic assumptions that must be understood and accepted, as explained in the following sections.

Environmental Emphasis

An FBA is based on principles of behavior analysis and therefore emphasizes the importance of the environment as the chief behavioral change agent. This fits well with a Response to Intervention perspective in that it allows for direct intervention with behavior and the measurement of behavior change (i.e., a response) as a result of the intervention.

Four Functions

An FBA focuses on four possible functions of behavior. Although many hypotheses about the "cause" of a given student's undesirable behavior may suggest apparent internal motivation (revenge, power, control, etc.), an FBA seeks to identify the relationship between the behavior and environment in a more external manner. It is generally agreed that there are four major functions of behavior—social attention, tangible reinforcement, escape, and sensory reinforcement (Iwata, Dorsey, Slifer, Bauman, & Richman, 1994). The goal of the assessment specialist conducting the FBA is to identify which of these functions may be maintaining the behavior. For example, a student who is frequently disruptive during class may do so to (1) gain access to social attention from peers and/or teachers, (2) gain access to preferred activities or objects (e.g., teacher gives the student something enjoyable to do to keep him or her "busy"), (3) be removed from the classroom (perhaps to avoid assigned work or being called on), or (4) experience the sensory stimulation of his or her disruptions (auditory sounds, visually apparent facial expressions of others, etc.). It is from this perspective that FBA seeks to describe the functional relationship between behaviors and their maintaining consequences.

Intervention Linked to Behavioral Function

After an FBA is completed, the goal is either to change the antecedent (trigger) to avoid having the behavior occur to begin with or to implement an intervention that is linked to the behavioral function. For example, the student who was disruptive may respond differently to verbal reprimands, depending on the function of the disruptive behavior. If the function of disruptive behavior was for attention from the teacher, a verbal reprimand may facilitate the behavior. If the function was to gain tangible rewards, the reprimand may serve as a punisher—but only if the tangible rewards were also withheld. Sometimes the process can become very complex. For example, the function of disruptive behavior may be to gain peer attention. In this case, the function is attention, but the teacher reprimand may have little impact (neither increasing nor decreasing the disruptive behavior) if the peer attention is still obtained. Figuring out precisely the correct function is crucial to the development of an individualized intervention plan.

An important consideration in addition to these three basic assumptions is expert training. Because the process can become very complex and requires a general mindset (i.e., a strong behavior analysis perspective), it can be an arduous process for some school personnel and problem-solving teams. However, there are many tools that can help with the process of identifying behavioral function(s).

Tools for Functional Assessment

Although there are many methods for collecting data, it is easy to remember the general class of data collection method using the acronym RIOT (records review, interview, observation, and test). Because the topic of this chapter is diagnostic tools, we therefore focus on the tools that are most reliably helpful for developing empirically supported hypotheses related to behavioral function (Steege & Watson, 2009). These tools come from the O part of the RIOT acronym—observation. These observation methods include frequency counting, description recording, and systematic, direct behavior observation recording.

Frequency Counting

To collect frequency data, an observer (often the classroom teacher) simply tallies the number of times an identified behavior occurs during selected time periods throughout the day. Before implementing an individualized intervention, it is important to determine the frequency at which the behavior occurs in the classroom. Frequency counts provide three advantages. First, in collecting these data, we are better able to understand the effects of an intervention on behavior by comparing the pre-intervention behavior levels to the post-intervention behavior levels. Second, collecting frequency count data can help identify the most likely times throughout the day that the behavior occurs. This information is useful in determining a good time for other school personnel (such as a school psychologist) to observe the behavior. Finally, the frequency count can allow for the identification of potential variables that may evoke the behavior.

Figure 3.4 is a behavior frequency recording log for a student named Eric, whose disruptive behavior is talking out of turn. The blank cells indicate that the student was under observation but no instance of the behavior occurred at that time. A cell with an X indicates that data were not collected during that time (perhaps because the teacher did not have time to collect data then, or because observation times were randomly chosen and that particular time was not an observation period). A reproducible recording log is in the appendix and on the CD that comes with this book.

By analyzing the data, it is apparent that Eric's talking-out behavior most commonly occurs during math and on Mondays and Tuesdays. In addition, this behavior appears to be least likely to occur during writing. This observation immediately allows numerous hypotheses to be developed related to Eric's behavior. In addition, if an independent observer wished to view the behavior, he or she would have a good indication about the best time to visit the classroom. The observer might note the differences in location, time of day, materials, class arrangements, and other variables that may be different between when the behavior does and does not occur.

It is important to point out that frequency recording may be a very helpful method for understanding how severe a behavior is and noting where it does and does not occur, but it does not inform our hypothesis about the cause (function) of the behavior. That is, based on the data in Figure 3.4, we cannot discern whether the behavior is being maintained by tangible reinforcement, attention, escape from academic demands, and/or sensory stimulation. Therefore, other methods of data collection are required in addition to frequency counting.

Behavior Description Recording

A second way to collect data that does help us identify potential behavioral function is behavior description recording (BDR; a reproducible form is in the appendix and on the CD that accompanies this book). A BDR also has a second advantage in that, when completed (commonly by the classroom teacher), it can provide school personnel an opportunity to record behavior of low frequency. When visiting a classroom in hope of observing a specific behavior, school personnel often find that it does not occur during the visit. That is because the behavior occurs at a low frequency, or the presence of the observer may cause a temporary change in the student's behavior. A BDR allows the teacher to record, in somewhat narrative form, when the behavior occurred, the setting, the task that should have been engaged in, the actual behavior, the consequence for the behavior, and what effect the consequence had.

Figure 3.5 is a an example of a BDR for a second-grade student named J. D. From the data, it is apparent that J. D. is not likely engaging in this low-frequency behavior (about once every other day or so) for sensory stimulation or tangible reinforcement. We draw this conclusion because J. D. does not receive anything tangible for his behavior nor is he engaging in the behavior when alone. It might be possible that the behavior serves the function of

FIGURE 3.4   **Example of a behavior frequency recording log.**

Behavior Frequency Recording Log

Student: Eric S.   Dates: 4/23–4/27

Behavior: Talking Out Without Permission   Observer: Meg T.

Start/End Times	Activity	Monday	Tuesday	Wednesday	Thursday	Friday
8:00–8:50	Reading	/ /	///	X		X
9:00–9:50	Math	//////	/////	//	////	//
10:00–10:50	Writing	/				
11:00–11:50	Social Studies		///	X	/	
12:00–12:50	Lunch and Recess				X	
1:00–1:50	Science	X	X	/		/
2:00–2:50	Specials	X	/	/	/	//

Observer Comments:
1. I used X's to indicate when no data were collected.
2. Blanks indicate no behavior despite observation.
3. This is worse than I thought. Help!

FIGURE 3.5   **Example of a behavior description recording log.**

BEHAVIOR DESCRIPTION RECORDING LOG

Directions: Please be as specific as possible.

Child's Name: J.D.   **Date:** 10/20
Grade: 2nd   **Teacher:** Mrs. Deaney
Setting: School: Library, classroom, recess   **Observer:** Mr. Lamb

Date	Time	Setting (where did the behavior take place?)	Task (what should student be doing?)	Behavior (what did student do?)	Consequences (how did you and/or other students react?)	Effect (what happened after these reactions?)
10/14	9:15	Library	Picking out a book	Pushed a peer	I sent him to the office	Came back and was polite
10/16	10:05	Small group art project	Working with peers	Threw glue bottle at peer	Given a time-out in the hall	Came back in, calm
10/17	9:45	Recess	Free play	Hit peer in face with small pebble	Stood him against wall; peer cried	Went to class with bad attitude
10/18	9:00	Classroom	Transitioning between reading and specials (today was computer skills)	Did not transition quietly	Reminded him he must transition quietly	He continued singing, "Don't you wish your girlfriend was hot like me?" and asking a peer about American Idol—he even asked if I watched it
10/19	10:45	Classroom	Working with peers on piñata	Pushed peer's work materials on the floor	Sent him to the office and called mother	His mother picked him up and took him home

Teacher Comments:

As you can see, he is often rude, does not respond well to traditional discipline, and is aggressive toward peers.

escape, because J. D. was allowed to leave the class (sent to the office, his mother picked him up, etc.). However, he may be engaging in the behavior for attention from peers, because after losing access to peer attention, the effect suggested that his behavior was "better." In other words, the removal of peer attention may serve as a time-out punishment.

Although the BDR has the advantage of identifying function for low-frequency behavior (and perhaps for high-frequency behavior as well), it has three limitations. First, it doesn't allow for a comparison to other peers. It is possible that other students engage in the same behavior patterns at the same frequency, but for some reason a particular student is being singled out. Second, it is not clear how systematically the behavior was recorded. It is possible that a teacher missed many of the behaviors, failed to record them, or simply was not consistent in defining the behavior. It is therefore important to use a method of data collection that addresses these issues.

Systematic, Direct Behavior Observation Recording

Systematic, direct behavior observation recording (SDBOR; a reproducible form is in the appendix and on the CD that accompanies this book) allows school personnel to obtain a severity ratio between the target student and his or her peers. In addition, it provides a reliable measurement of the behavior from someone who is not simultaneously burdened with collecting data and trying to manage a classroom full of students while instructing. Figure 3.6 is an example of a direct behavior observation recording log. Each box represents a 30-second observation interval. An X in the box indicates that the behavior occurred. If there is no X, the behavior did not occur.

Notice there are two sets of data on the recording log in Figure 3.6. One is for the target student; the other set of boxes is for a "composite" student. The composite student is established by systematically alternating between observing the target student and observing each peer within the classroom. This alternating is done until each student in the classroom is observed at least once following an observation interval of the target student being observed. To get an estimate of severity, one can simply calculate the discrepancy between the target student and the composite student. For example, Figure 3.6 shows that the target student, Ryan, is engaged in talking-out behavior during 12 of the 40 intervals (30 percent), while the composite student engaged in the behavior during 5 of the 40 intervals (12.5 percent). The discrepancy ratio in this case is 2.4 (30 percent divided by 12.5 percent, or 12 occurrences divided by 5 occurrences). This means that Ryan is engaged in talking-out behavior 2.4 times more often than the composite peer. As a rule of thumb, a student who is engaged in problem behavior at a level two times greater than that of his or her respective peers warrants intervention. However, if the student is not at least two times discrepant, the teacher may want to consider intervention at a small-group or classroom level. By having initial discrepancy data, educators can use a discrepancy ratio as a means of evaluating an intervention while monitoring progress over time.

SUMMARY OF IMPORTANT POINTS

This chapter provided a foundation for understanding diagnostic tools and procedures for Tiers II and III. After reading this chapter, you are encouraged to study Chapter 7, which addresses important considerations and lessons learned that you are likely to find helpful in understanding and navigating the challenges that come with choosing and utilizing diag-

FIGURE 3.6   Example of a systematic behavior observation recording log.

<u>Behavior Observation Recording Log</u>

Target Student Name: <u>Ryan C.</u>   **Birth date:** <u>4/1/98</u>
School: <u>Lincoln Elementary</u>   **Teacher:** <u>Mr. Mitchell</u>
Observer: <u>Sara A.</u>   **Date:** <u>5/30</u>

Behavior(s)	Definitions
Behavior 1: Aggression (A)	Physical or verbal actions toward another person that has potential for harm
Behavior 2: Talk-outs (TO)	Verbalizations without permission
Behavior 3: On-task (OT)	Oriented to academic task or appropriate engagement with materials
Behavior 4:	
Behavior 5:	

Target Child (TC)

Behavior	1	2	3	4	5	6	7	8	9	10	11	12	13	14	15	16	17	18	19	20
1 A								X						X						
2 TO	X			X				X	X					X				X		
3 OT	X	X	X		X	X	X		X	X	X	X	X		X	X	X	X	X	X
4																				
5																				

Behavior	21	22	23	24	25	26	27	28	29	30	31	32	33	34	35	36	37	38	39	40
1 A				X										X						
2 TO		X	X			X						X				X				X
3 OT	X				X					X					X		X			
4																				
5																				

Composite Child (CC)

Behavior	1	2	3	4	5	6	7	8	9	10	11	12	13	14	15	16	17	18	19	20
1 A						X														
2 TO	X									X									X	
3 OT	X	X	X	X	X	X	X	X	X		X	X	X	X	X	X	X	X		X
4																				
5																				

Behavior	21	22	23	24	25	26	27	28	29	30	31	32	33	34	35	36	37	38	39	40
1 A																				
2 TO				X												X				
3 OT	X	X	X	X	X	X	X	X			X	X	X	X	X		X	X	X	X
4																				
5																				

TCB1 <u>4/40</u>   TCB2 <u>12/40</u>   TCB3 <u>22/40</u>   TCB4 _____   TCB5 _____
CCB1 <u>1/40</u>   CCB2 <u>5/40</u>   CCB3 <u>35/40</u>   CCB4 _____   CCB5 _____

Note:
TCB1, TCB2, etc. = Target Child Behavior 1, Target Child Behavior 2, etc.
CCB1, CCB2, etc. = Composite Child Behavior 1, Composite Child Behavior 2, etc.
To calculate percentages: (No. of Occurrences ÷ No. of Observations) × 100 = %.
For example, if there were 4 occurrences in 40 observations, (4 ÷ 40) × 100 = 10%

nostic tools and procedures (reporting results, training personnel, selection, linking to intervention, etc.). The following are important points about diagnostic tools and procedures to be stressed with those individuals you may be working with in the early stages of implementation.

◻ **Diagnostic tools have three purposes.** Diagnostic tools are used to (1) follow up on results of universal screening measures, (2) identify skills deficits, and (3) facilitate linking students to needed services.

□ **Diagnostic tools have four common characteristics.** A diagnostic tool is often administered in a one-to-one format. A DT requires more time to administer than a universal screening measure. A DT generally contains a larger sample of items and has a wider variety of items than a USM.

□ **DT-A procedures may differ at Tiers II and III.** Although the same types of assessments for DT-A at Tier II may be used for DT-A at Tier III, Tier III DT-As typically require more analysis of response patterns, similar to that used with curriculum-based evaluation.

□ **DT-B procedures may differ at Tiers II and III.** Although rating scales are often used for DT-Bs at Tier II, more intensive procedures are used at Tier III. These include functional behavior assessment and analysis, which focuses on the systematic identification of environmental variables that may evoke or maintain the target behavior(s). This process often requires specialized training in behavior analysis most often obtained from a special educator or school psychologist.

□ **Diagnostic tools are not the only data to consider.** Diagnostic tools are used as only one source of data. It is important to use RIOT (records review, interview, observation, and test) and obtain at least two data sources before making a determination about whether to provide services at a more intense level.

REFERENCES

Achenbach, T. (2010). *The Achenbach System of Empirically Based Assessment.* www.aseba.org

Connoly, A. J. (2008). *KeyMath3™ Diagnostic Assessment.* http://psychcorp.pearsonassessments.com/HAIWEB/Cultures/en-us/Productdetail.htm?Pid=PAaKeymath3

Howell, K. W., & Nolet, V. (2000). *Curriculum-based evaluation: Teaching and decision making* (3rd ed.). Belmont, CA: Wadsworth.

Iwata, B. A., Dorsey, M. F., Slifer, K. J., Bauman, K. E., & Richman, G. S. (1994). Toward a functional analysis of self injury. *Journal of Applied Behavior Analysis, 27,* 197–209 (Reprinted from *Analysis and Intervention in Developmental Disabilities, 2,* 3–20, 1982)

Kamphaus, R. W., & Reynolds, C. (2009). *BASC™-2 Behavior Assessment System for Children* (2nd ed.). San Antonio, TX: Pearson Education.

Steege, M. W., & Watson, T. S. (2009). *Conducting school-based functional behavioral assessments* (2nd ed.). New York, NY: Guilford Press.

Walker, H., & Severson, H. H. (1991). *Systematic Screening for Behavior Disorders.* Longmont, CO: Sopris West.

Wright, J. (May, 2010). *Math Probe Generator.* http://jimwrightonline.com/htmdocs/tools/mathprobe/addsing.php

RECOMMENDED RESOURCES

Information, Tools, and Services for Improving Academic Performance and Social Behavior

www.garycates.com

CHAPTER 4

Monitoring Student Performance Through the RTI Process

CHAPTER OVERVIEW

Monitoring student progress is an essential hallmark in the implementation of an effective Response to Intervention system. This chapter aids in understanding progress monitoring for both academic performance and social behavior. It seeks to build on and support the objectives of previous chapters. Specifically this chapter will:

- ☐ Discuss the purpose and rationale for monitoring progress.
- ☐ Discuss the characteristics of progress monitoring tools.
- ☐ Discuss the frequency and focus of monitoring progress at each tier.
- ☐ Describe data-based decision making with progress monitoring tools for academic performance.
- ☐ Describe data-based decision making with progress monitoring tools for social behavior.
- ☐ Provide recommended resources and references for further use and understanding.

PURPOSE OF AND RATIONALE FOR MONITORING PROGRESS

Monitoring student progress is an essential component of the implementation process of any RTI model. By monitoring performance in the areas of reading, writing, math, and social behavior, intervention specialists can determine student responsiveness to intervention at any tier. If students are responding favorably, intervention may be maintained or begun to be systematically faded. If students are not responding favorably, then more-intensive service is provided and/or a change in the type of intervention is made. By continually monitoring student progress, school personnel can ensure that students receive an appropriate level and type of instructional support.

CHARACTERISTICS OF THE PROGRESS MONITORING PROCESS

A progress monitoring tool (PMT) shares many of the same characteristics as a universal screening measure (USM). Specifically, a PMT should (1) be brief to administer, (2) allow for multiple administrations and repeated measurement of student performance, and (3) be simple to score and interpret. Although PMTs are commonly administered individually, they may also be administered to groups of students simultaneously.

PMTs for Academic Performance

PMTs for academic performance (PMT-A) often resemble the curriculum-based measurements (sometimes referred to as probes) that are readily available from DIBELS®, AIMSweb®, and easyCBM®. The National Center on Student Progress Monitoring (see Recommended Resources at the end of this chapter) provides a review of many commonly used PMTs. The staff responsible for RTI planning and implementation might wish to refer to this review when selecting a PMT.

It should be pointed out that PMT-As used at Tier II are generally the same as those used at Tier III. The PMT-A data collected at both Tier II and Tier III are often displayed in a graph. ChartDog is a free, online chart maker that is useful for this purpose (see Recommended Resources at the end of this chapter).

PMTs for Social Behavior

PMTs for social behavior (PMT-B) at Tier II usually are forms to be filled out by school personnel responsible for the collection of behavior data. (See Chapter 3 for a discussion of these forms.) Although the PMT-Bs used at Tiers II and III may be the same, like PMT-As, the data are often recorded in a graph.

FREQUENCY AND FOCUS OF MONITORING PROGRESS AT EACH TIER

Tier I Progress Monitoring

The focus of Tier I is on prevention of academic and social behavior problems and maintenance of current performance of students not identified as being at risk. This prevention and maintenance can be accomplished simply through use of a USM. Specifically, educators should focus on maintaining the performance of any student not identified as at risk given the cut scores (benchmarks) on USM-As and USM-Bs. However, students who begin to perform below cut-score levels should be provided additional support—after further screening and/or diagnostic assessment—in order to prevent the area of concern from becoming worse. Tier I progress monitoring (universal screening) should occur three times per year.

Tier II Progress Monitoring

The focus of Tier II is to provide standard protocol interventions to students at risk of not meeting predetermined expectations. Students receiving additional support at the Tier II level therefore receive additional monitoring of progress beyond the three universal screenings per year in order to determine whether the standard protocol intervention is resulting in improved performance. Progress monitoring at Tier II should occur about once per week.

Tier III Progress Monitoring

The focus of Tier III is to provide individualized intervention to students who have not made adequate progress toward meeting expectations despite receiving standard protocol intervention. Students receiving individualized Tier III intervention should therefore receive additional monitoring of their progress beyond that provided at the Tier II level. Because the severity of the problem is greater at Tier III, it is important to monitor progress more frequently—at least twice per week.

DATA-BASED DECISION MAKING WITH PROGRESS MONITORING TOOLS FOR ACADEMIC PERFORMANCE

After collecting data with a PMT, school personnel are charged with analyzing, interpreting, and responding to the information. These data-based decisions are generally made through analysis of graphs. This analysis is a hallmark of RTI and is most common at the individual student level; therefore, it is an everyday task for any school that implements RTI.

What school personnel monitor specifically is the progress a student (or group of students) has made toward a predetermined goal. Therefore, before monitoring student progress, it is important to define the goal for which progress will be assessed. At the Tier I level, this goal is simply meeting benchmarks. At the Tier II, Tier III, and special education levels, goals are set with regard to the progress made toward specific benchmarks. This can be accomplished by assessing improvement relative to peers and toward specific criteria.

Rate of Improvement Relative to Peers

One of the most common and simplest ways of setting a goal is to use the rate of improvement of same-grade peers. Rate of improvement (ROI) can be defined as the average amount of gain per week. For example, say the USM-A is oral reading fluency (ORF) for a given second-grade class and that the fall benchmark average on the ORF is 62. Let's also say that 15 weeks later, the average is now 77. The average ROI in this case is one word correct per minute increase per week (i.e., 15 words gained in 15 weeks).

By knowing the average ROI, educators can be better equipped in setting goals. If peers are progressing at an average of one word correct per minute increase per week on ORF, the goal for a student receiving services at Tier II may be set at the same rate such that the gap between peers and the target student does not become larger. However, to close the gap between the target student and his or her respective peers, an ROI greater than one word correct per minute per week increase would be needed (i.e., more than a 15-word gain in the 15 weeks).

The following is an example of using peer ROI. Figure 4.1 represents the progress of a student who is currently reading 45 words correct per minute and who is going to receive 15 weeks of service at the Tier II level. The dashed line represents the average rate of improvement from one benchmarking period to the next. This line is the "goal" for struggling learners. The solid line represents the student's actual performance. This line is

FIGURE 4.1   **An example of setting goals based on average peer rate of improvement.**

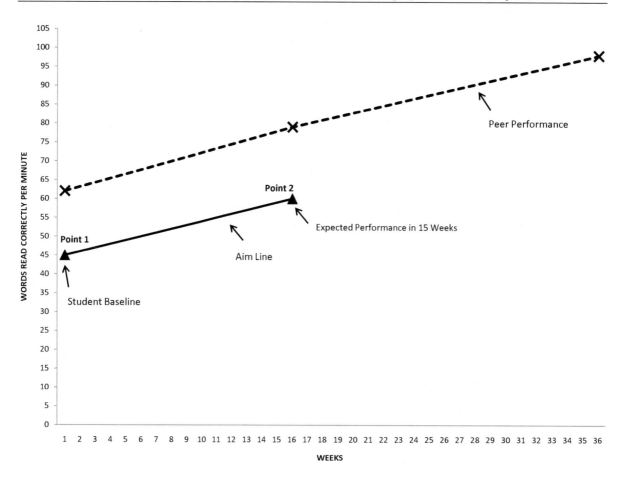

referred to as the aim line. An aim line is a trajectory of a student's expected rate of improvement on a graph if the intervention goal is to maintain the rate of improvement of a student equal to his or her peers. Point one on the solid line is where the target student is performing at the initial benchmarking period. Point two represents where the student will need to be in order to keep the gap from becoming wider.

We know that the target student's peers have been gaining about one word correct per minute increase per week. We can therefore do a bit of simple math to determine where the student should be in 15 weeks.

Current performance level + (# of weeks in intervention × expected rate of improvement)

In our current example, we simply can plug in the numbers:

$$45 + (15 \times 1) = 60$$

In 15 weeks, we would expect the target student to be reading 60 words correct per minute if our intervention is helping the student achieve the same rate of improvement as everyone else. To determine whether the intervention is working, we could simply ask ourselves at the end of the 15 weeks, "Did the student meet our expected rate of performance?" This method of goal setting ensures that the student maintains an adequate rate of growth without falling further behind.

What becomes immediately apparent is that if we set the target student's rate of improvement goal as one word correct per minute increase per week, we can expect the student to make progress at least at the same rate as his or her peers. However, the gap still exists. It is advisable to set more-ambitious goals such that the gap between the target student and his or her respective peers closes. Figure 4.2 is an example of what an aim line would look like if an ambitious goal of two words correct per minute increase per week would have been set in the previous example. Shapiro (2008) provides recommendations for ambitious goals for grades 1 through 6.

Although comparing target student performance to peer performance is an acceptable method for setting goals, there is one important limitation to this method. Setting goals relative to peers does not consider improvement relative to educational learning standards. It is possible in a low-performing school (where students are doing poorly compared to a national average) to have a student close the gap but still not meet educational standards. Moreover, in a high-performing school (where many students meet expectations on high-stakes tests), it is possible to have expectations that are higher than necessary for a target student to achieve educational learning standards.

Rate of Improvement Toward Criterion

An alternative way of setting goals that is in line with a standards-based expectation is to compare student performance to an expected outcome at a specific point in time. Figure 4.3 represents the progress of a student who is currently reading 45 words correct per minute and who is going to receive 15 weeks of service at the Tier II level. We know that in order to comfortably predict that the student will make adequate yearly progress (i.e., meet expectations on a high-stakes test), he or she must be reading 79 words correct per minute at the end of the 15 weeks. We therefore do not need to calculate the rate of improvement. We simply draw a line from current performance to expected performance with the appropriate amount of time on the *x* axis between the two points. Note that, given these numbers, the graph will look like the one in Figure 4.2. The primary difference is that we are comparing the target student to where we would like him or her to be (meeting expectations) rather than to the performance of peers (who may or may not be meeting expectations).

Although the ROI relative to a criterion method can guard against setting goals that are too low or too high for target students, it has a disadvantage as well. The disadvantage is that the criterion may be too lofty for a given student. This disadvantage is likely to be less pronounced at lower grades because, in theory, the amount of gap between a student and his or her peers should be smaller early in the educational career than it would be later. Therefore, we recommend using the criterion method for younger students and the peer method for older students—that is, set lofty goals when students are younger so that moderate goals are needed down the road. Prevention of problems is a hallmark of RTI.

MONITORING PROGRESS ALONG THE WAY

Simply evaluating pre-intervention and post-intervention performance is not sufficient. It is important to monitor progress *during* the intervention as well because adjustment of the intervention may sometimes be necessary. Using a graph with an aim line can be very valuable because it allows school personnel to plot a student's weekly performance data

FIGURE 4.2 **Example of closing the gap by setting ambitious goals relative to average peer rate of improvement.**

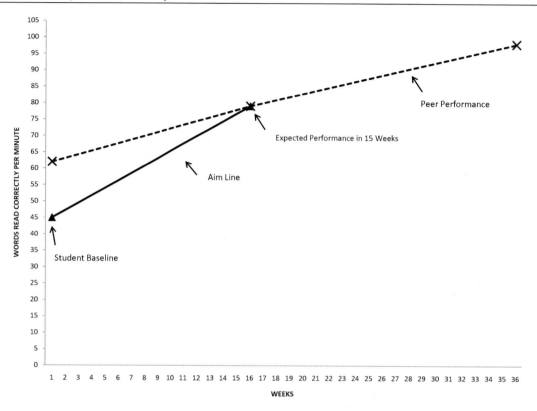

FIGURE 4.3 **Example of criterion-based goal setting.**

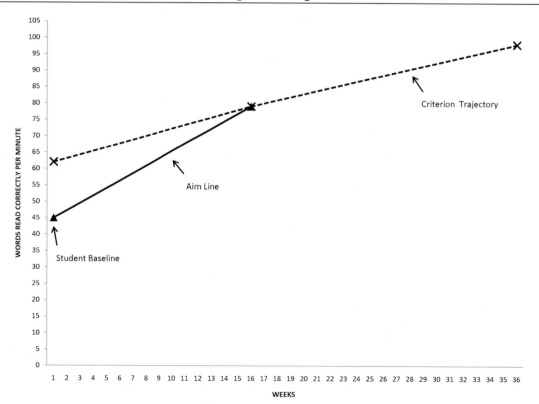

relative to the aim line. By drawing a line of best fit through student performance, we can compare the student's expected rate of performance aim line with the actual rate of improvement, or trend line. A trend line can easily be obtained from many of the data management programs such as AIMSweb and Microsoft Excel®. Once we have both the aim line (the expected rate of improvement) and the trend line (the actual rate of improvement), we can make both formative and summative decisions. Summative decisions require waiting until the end of a pre-specified length of time to evaluate the entire outcome of the intervention, whereas summative decisions can be made prior to the end of the pre-specified evaluation date.

SUMMATIVE DECISIONS (CHANGING INTERVENTIONS)

A common question among school personnel implementing RTI is "How long must an intervention be implemented before determining whether it is effective?" The answer we often provide to this question is "However long the intervention manual recommends." For some Tier II standard protocol interventions, this period is often specified. However, for other Tier II interventions and many individualized interventions that are developed "in house," there is no manual. In these cases, it is important to follow the guidelines that are available from empirical research on visual inspection of data. Specifically, it is recommended that 10 to 15 data points are needed in order to make reliable (i.e., consistent) judgments with regard to intervention effectiveness (Kazdin, 1982). This 10- to 15-data-points rule of thumb for intervention implementation translates into an intervention being implemented at the Tier II level for approximately 10 to 15 weeks (assuming data are collected once per week). Although benchmarking may occur closer to 15 weeks apart, quarter grades and other data commonly collected may occur closer to a 10-week interval. The important point is that the amount of time that elapses between benchmarking assessments and/or the end of quarters typically approximates this range, which allows for additional data to be considered in conjunction with the progress monitoring data when making decisions.

When no intervention manual is available, it is recommended that changes in intervention be made at the end of some pre-specified evaluation date (sometimes at the end of a quarter and the end of a benchmarking period). Making changes before this time may violate recommendations that are set forth by a manual and/or not allow for enough data to be collected to make a reliable decision about intervention effectiveness.

Slope/Trend Rules

When making decisions about effectiveness, it is important to consider the slope of the trend line relative to the goal and/or aim line. The steeper the slope of the trend line relative to the aim line or goal line, the more effective the intervention is considered to be. There are essentially three possible outcomes when comparing slopes; therefore, there are essentially three possible decisions.

Data-Point Decision 1

If the student trend line is flatter than the aim line, consider adjusting or changing the intervention. Figure 4.4 is an example of this scenario.

FIGURE 4.4   **Example of an aim line steeper than a trend line, resulting in a decision to change and/or intensify the intervention.**

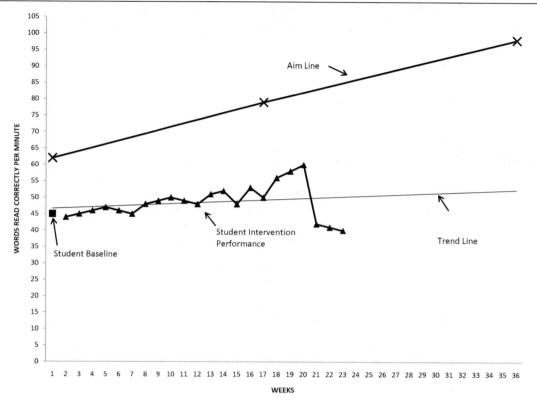

Data-Point Decision 2

If the student's trend line is steeper than the aim line, consider moving down a tier (i.e., begin to fade the intervention). Figure 4.5 is an example of this scenario.

Data-Point Decision 3

If the student's trend line is roughly the same as the aim line, continue or intensify the intervention. Figure 4.6 is an example of this scenario.

FORMATIVE DECISIONS (ADJUSTING INTERVENTIONS)

Although making decisions about the overall outcome of an intervention is important in determining whether an intervention should be maintained, abandoned, substituted, or intensified, sometimes it is also important to make adjustments. These adjustments are minor modifications to interventions made before the pre-specified evaluation date. The minor changes may include such things as changes in font size of printed material, changing where the interventionist sits relative to the target student, and having the student use a ruler to keep from skipping lines while reading orally. These adjustments are modifications to the current intervention and do not require any instructional modifications. The intervention itself remains the same.

FIGURE 4.5 **Example of a trend line steeper than an aim line, resulting in a decision to fade the intervention.**

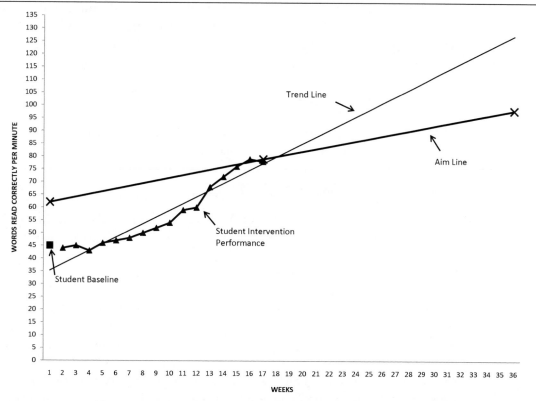

FIGURE 4.6 **Example of a trend line roughly equal to the aim line, resulting in a decision to continue or intensify the intervention.**

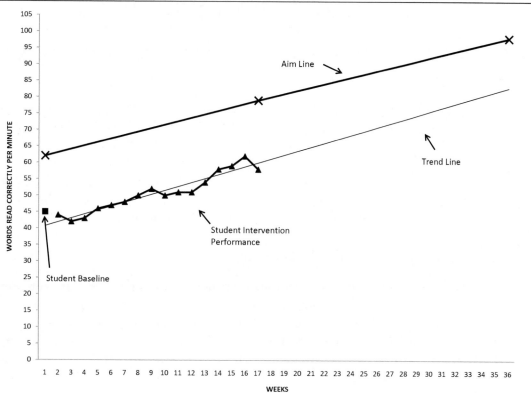

Three Data-Point Decision Rules

To make these decisions, we rely on analyzing, at minimum, the most recent three data points because three data points are the minimum required for a trend (Kazdin, 1982). Given the three data-point rule, three outcomes are possible; therefore, one of three decisions can be made at a given time.

Three Data-Point Decision Rule 1

If there are three consecutive data points *below* the aim line, then an adjustment may be made. Figure 4.7 is an example of this scenario.

Three Data-Point Decision Rule 2

If there are three consecutive data points *above* the aim line, then a reduction in the frequency of the intervention can also be made. Figure 4.8 is an example of this scenario.

Three Data-Point Decision Rule 3

If there are not three consecutive data points above or below the aim line, then no adjustment should be made. Figure 4.9 is an example of this scenario.

When making adjustments to interventions, it should be noted that the adjustments should be left in place until the three data-point rule again applies. That is, once an adjustment has been made, it should not be removed or another adjustment made until a trend (three consecutive data points above or below the aim line) has been established.

It should be clear that data-based decision making requires an adherence to rules. By adhering to these rules, school personnel can ensure that they remain objective and treat all students in a consistent manner.

DATA-BASED DECISION MAKING WITH PROGRESS MONITORING TOOLS FOR SOCIAL BEHAVIOR

Although there have been a few studies (Cheney, Flower, & Templeton, 2008; Cheney et al., 2009; Fairbanks, Sugai, Guardino, & Lathrop, 2008; Hawken, MacLeod, & Rawlings, 2007; Walker, Cheney, Stage, Blum, & Horner, 2005) on RTI and criteria for decision making when a social behavior is the targeted learning goal, our understanding of what criteria should be used is still limited. However, the practices discussed earlier in this chapter about PMTs for academic performance have long been used in behavioral evaluation and are therefore useful when making decisions about behavior.

Tier II Progress Monitoring Tool

Once a student is identified through diagnostic tools and office discipline referrals (discussed in Chapters 2 and 3) as needing additional Tier II support, monitoring the effects of this support is required. At the Tier II level of support, the primary focus is on a standard protocol intervention. The Tier II intervention often utilizes a feedback and reward system that is monitored using a daily behavior report (DBR) card. Researchers have found that the DBR, when used properly, can be a valid indicator of

FIGURE 4.7 Example of three consecutive data points below the aim line, resulting in a decision to adjust administration of an intervention.

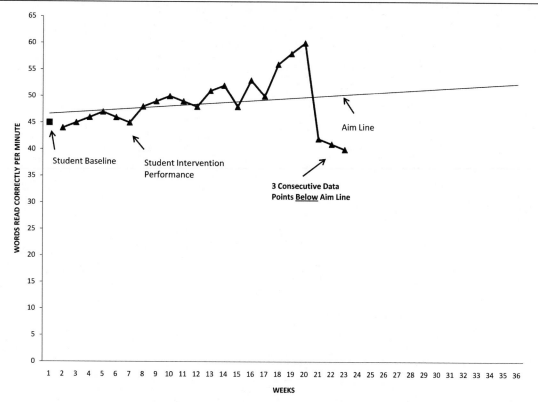

FIGURE 4.8 Example of three consecutive data points above the aim line, resulting in a decision to reduce frequency of an intervention.

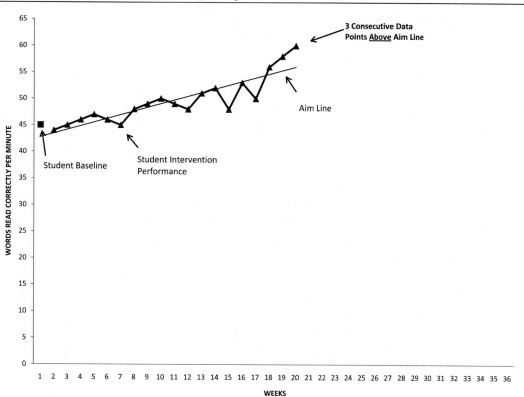

FIGURE 4.9   **Example of three data points (none consecutive), indicating that no adjustment to the intervention should be made.**

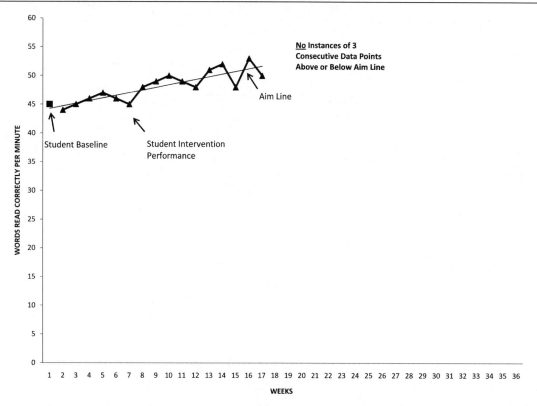

critical behaviors relevant to Tier II progress (Chafouleas, McDougal, Riley-Tillman, Panahon, & Hilt, 2005; Chafouleas, Riley-Tillman, Sassu, LaFrance, & Patwa, 2007; Cheney et al., 2008; Fabiano, Vujnovic, Naylor, Pariseau, & Robins, 2009). Although there are many approaches, one of the most successful methods is to rate student progress on schoolwide behavior expectations. Specifically, students are required to have their teachers rate their behavioral performance with regard to the behavior expectations delineated at the school. An example of schoolwide expectations and a daily behavior report card reflecting these expectations is provided in Figure 4.10. A free DBR generator is available online (see Recommended Resources at the end of this chapter; in addition, an Excel template for recording and charting behavior data is available on the CD that accompanies this book).

Once a problem-solving team has ensured that their DBRs are a good match for their Tier II intervention and that everyone understands protocol and is following it, it becomes possible to make meaningful decisions based on the data generated. Like academic data, for behavioral data to be used effectively in a comprehensive RTI model, it must be tracked and graphed. This can be done using Microsoft Excel or a program with special features designed specifically for a behavior education program (BEP). It should also be noted that user-friendly commercial tools designed specifically for this purpose, such as the Check-In/Check-Out (CICO) School-Wide Information System, available from the University of Oregon, are available (May, Talmadge, Todd, Horner, & Rossetto-Dickey, 2009).

FIGURE 4.10   **Example of a daily behavior report card.**

DAILY BEHAVIOR REPORT CARD

Date: _____   Teacher: _____   Student: _____

0 = No   1 = Yes

	Be Safe	Be Respectful	Be Ready		Teacher Initials
	Keep hands, feet, and objects to self	Use kind words and actions	Follow directions	Have needed materials	
Reading	0 1	0 1	0 1	0 1	
Recess	0 1	0 1	0 1	0 1	
Math	0 1	0 1	0 1	0 1	
Lunch	0 1	0 1	0 1	0 1	
Social Studies	0 1	0 1	0 1	0 1	
Recess	0 1	0 1	0 1	0 1	
Language Arts	0 1	0 1	0 1	0 1	
Science	0 1	0 1	0 1	0 1	

Total Points = _____   Today _____ %   Goal _____ %

Points possible = 32

Parent/guardian signature _____

Making data-based decisions using daily report cards for social behavior may require that students maintain established criteria levels for sustained periods of time before being released from a BEP. As seen in Figure 4.11, the student, Patty, has had four days when she fell below the criterion set at 80 percent. The problem-solving team may want to extend Patty's participation in the program because she is responding to it but is still having some days of difficulty. If Patty is released from the program too soon, the team faces the risk of her problem behaviors recurring. At the same time, because she is responding, there seems to be no need for Tier III interventions. The daily report card also allows the observer to indicate when data were not collected or when the student was absent. (A template for the daily behavior report card is available in the appendix and on the accompanying CD.)

If a student has sustained progress to the point where he or she is meeting the established criteria on the daily behavior report card and receiving no ODRs, it may be time to fade the intervention. In a behavior education program, it is recommended that the student be put on self-monitoring intervention to ease the transition for the student and encourage independence.

FIGURE 4.11   **Example of daily behavior report card for monitoring student progress.**

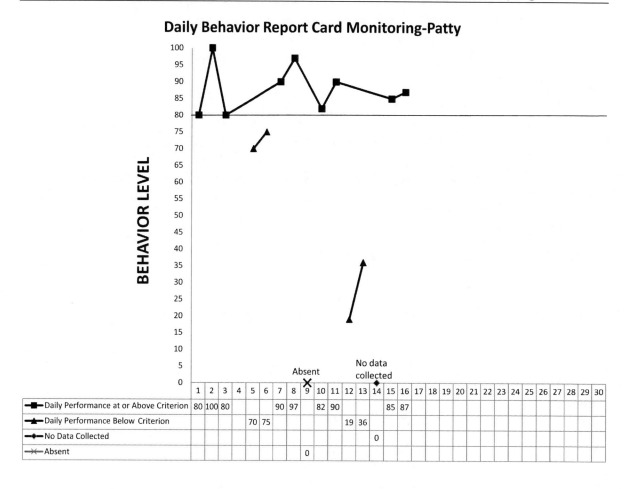

On the other hand, some students clearly may not respond to the Tier II intervention—in this case, the BEP (Crone, Hawken, & Horner, 2010). As seen in Figure 4.12, although it appeared that there was an initial response to the BEP, Patty has fallen well below the criterion for 7 days. This should be a red flag for the problem-solving team that the Tier II intervention for behavior may not be working. Although Patty is not receiving ODRs during the time period, if she keeps performing this poorly in class on behavioral expectations, it is a matter of time before ODRs begin to recur.

In this case, it may be best for the problem-solving team to consider a Tier III intervention—typically, some form of functional behavior assessment and multicomponent individualized positive behavior support plan. The details of monitoring and identifying the function of behavior using this approach in a Tier III intervention are discussed in Chapters 3 and 6. However, although Tier III for behavior support may require specialized data and assessment approaches, progress monitoring, and making data-based decisions in problem-solving teams, it is consistent at all three levels of intervention for both academic performance and social behavior. As discussed in Chapter 3, graphing student progress is an essential part of data-based decision making for problem-solving teams. Whether you are using Microsoft Excel or a dedicated program, data should be visually depicted to help a problem-solving team make sound decisions.

FIGURE 4.12   **Daily behavior report card showing decreasing trends in following behavioral expectations.**

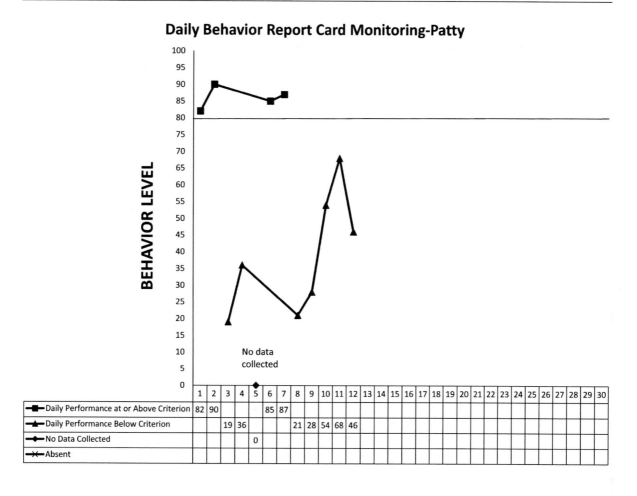

Daily Behavior Report Card Monitoring-Patty

	1	2	3	4	5	6	7	8	9	10	11	12	13	14	15	16	17	18	19	20	21	22	23	24	25	26	27	28	29	30
■ Daily Performance at or Above Criterion	82	90				85	87																							
▲ Daily Performance Below Criterion			19	36				21	28	54	68	46																		
◆ No Data Collected					0																									
✕ Absent																														

We discussed daily behavior report cards in the context of one popularized approach to Tier II interventions for social behavior problems. However, DBRs can be used with almost any Tier II intervention as long as their use is aligned with desired outcomes of that particular intervention. For example, if the school uses a social problem-solving approach as a Tier II intervention, and if the DBRs include critical outcomes that were intended by the problem-solving curriculum, monitoring student progress will be useful. However, the criteria that should be used for responding to the intervention and for determining failure to respond should be based on the recommendations of the program developer. Some interventions may take longer before they are judged ineffective. Other interventions may take only a couple of weeks to determine effectiveness.

Finally, in a comprehensive model of RTI, academic performance and social behavior should not be considered alone. Data-based decision making needs to be an integrated process in which a problem-solving team considers all of the data.

EVALUATING THE RTI MODEL

Accountability is emphasized through legislation such as No Child Left Behind and the Individuals with Disabilities Education Improvement Act (see Chapter 1 for more information about these laws). To be consistent with these laws and to ensure a successful problem-solving initiative in your school, the RTI process should be evaluated. This evaluation should include assessing student outcomes associated with problem solving. These results should be distributed to all stakeholders, including school staff and parents.

Formative and Summative Evaluation

Evaluation should be both formative and summative. Formative assessment occurs during the first few years of implementation and permits the school to make decisions and change its problem-solving practices throughout the school year. The goal of providing this feedback is to improve the problem-solving process in order to reach the goal of improving outcomes for all students.

Summative evaluation, occurring after the process has been implemented at least 3 to 5 years, allows the school to make conclusions about the success of the problem-solving efforts at the end of that time period. The evaluation should focus on the problem-solving process, consumer satisfaction, and student outcomes.

Process Variables

When assessing process, questions to be answered include the following:

◻ How many staff are trained?

◻ Who are they serving?

◻ What types of problems are the problem-solving teams at the different tiers addressing?

◻ Is the problem-solving process being implemented with integrity?

◻ What is the quality of implementation?

◻ Does the process have all of the recommended components?

◻ Are interventions being implemented with integrity?

◻ How are meetings being facilitated?

Self- and External Assessment

We have customarily evaluated process variables in two ways. First, we often utilize an RTI team self-assessment of the problem-solving implementation (SAPSI). This self-assessment is typically filled out by the RTI building-level team and is broad with regard to the components of effective implementation of RTI. The domains that we typically target in such a self-assessment include:

◻ Developing comprehensive system and support variables.

◻ Establishing and maintaining team processes.

◻ Implementing the three-tiered system.

◻ Implementing evidence-based practices.

◻ Monitoring and planning the RTI process at all three tiers.

Each domain has several subindicators of effective implementation that are also considered. For example, the domain of "developing comprehensive system and support variables" might include subindicators such as "adequate training has been provided to all educators and support personnel" and "there is sufficient administrator support for the development of an RTI system."

Second, and in addition to the SAPSI, we use an objective means to measure RTI implementation. Because the SAPSI-type assessment is based on the building team's collective perception, it is possible that the assessment could be inaccurate or biased. By having an external evaluator (e.g., someone from another school within the district or from another district) check for fidelity of the process using a similar evaluation tool, the building-level team can identify areas that may be in need of improvement as well as areas in which they may perceive their performance more favorably than an objective outsider does. The SAPSI and the objective fidelity tool can be found on the Loyola University Center for School Evaluation, Intervention & Training website (see Recommended Resources at the end of this chapter; the program was funded by a federal grant that focused on the implementation of RTI in the state of Illinois). Another method of evaluation is the Essential Elements Matrices (Johnson-Gros, Kaase, Medley, Cates, & Doggett, 2011).

Administrative Feedback

As with the evaluation of variables for the entire RTI process, it is also important to evaluate the problem-solving process in detail. Chapter 5 discusses all of the major components and variables important to effective and efficient problem solving. At this point, though, it is important only to point out that an assessment of this subprocess should be conducted by the building principal. In essence, the building principal observes the Tier III problem-solving team in action with a case or two. Using a checklist or feedback form enables the principal to objectively identify and provide feedback about the problem-solving team's strengths and weaknesses.

Parent Updates and Satisfaction

It is important to keep parents informed of student performance at all levels of the RTI process. Although most parents can be updated about their child's performance on the Tier I universal screening measure at parent–teacher conferences, parents or guardians with students receiving support at Tier II or Tier III may require more frequent updates. In addition, consumer satisfaction can be assessed through open-ended questions on parent and staff surveys. Examples of open-ended questions that may be asked of staff include the following:

◻ If you used problem-solving this year, what do you think worked well?

◻ What could be improved?

◻ If you did not use problem solving, why?

◻ What are some suggestions you have to make problem solving more effective?

Arguably, one of the most important stakeholders in the RTI process are parents and guardians. An example of a parent/guardian satisfaction survey can found on the Illinois ASPIRE website (see Recommended Resources at the end of this chapter).

Student Outcome Variables

Student outcomes represent a critical source of data, which should be part of any formative or summative evaluation of RTI. These outcomes should focus on the whole school or grade level and include student outcomes such as:

◻ Percentage of students in the school who are meeting expectations on state-mandated tests.

◻ Number of students retained at particular grade levels.

◻ Number of discipline referrals to the school office.

◻ Number of student absences.

◻ Frequency of more-severe behavioral infractions such as fighting.

Individual student outcomes should also focus on the number of students adequately or inadequately responding to interventions. A "Chutes and Ladders" analysis chart is an effective tool for monitoring this type of data. A Microsoft Excel template for that chart can be found on the Measured Effects website (see Recommended Resources at the end of this chapter).

These student outcome data can be used to determine the extent to which the RTI model adopted is successful. Any student outcome variable that is deemed to be at an unsatisfactory level or rate should be targeted for improvement. This may be best accomplished by considering these student outcome variables in relation to the process variables.

SUMMARY OF IMPORTANT POINTS

This chapter provided a foundation for monitoring student progress in an RTI framework in addition to suggestions for evaluating an RTI model. After reading this chapter, you are encouraged to study the final chapter of this book, which addresses important considerations and lessons learned that you are likely to find helpful in understanding and navigating the challenges that come with progress monitoring and program evaluation. The following are important points related to evaluation of RTI implementation and interventions.

◻ **Monitoring progress is an essential component of RTI.** RTI requires the monitoring of student performance using instruments that are similar to universal screening measures (USM). The data from progress monitoring should be graphed and shared with all relevant parties (students, teachers, parents/guardians). The frequency of progress monitoring is related to the tier being monitored. Tier I is monitored with benchmarking (USM) three times per year. Tier II is monitored at least once per week, and Tier III progress monitoring occurs at least two times per week.

◻ **The rate of improvement must be evaluated.** Progress monitoring is essentially the method used to evaluate a student's or group of students' rate of improvement. This rate of improvement can be understood best when compared to the typical peer rate of improvement or relative to the expected rate of improvement needed to meet a predetermined criterion.

◻ **All decision making should be data based.** The rate of improvement relative to peers or toward a criterion is used to make the decision with regard to both formative and summative decisions. Although formative decisions require analysis of three data points before an adjustment (such as a minor accommodation or change) to an intervention should be made, at least 10 to 15 data points are often suggested for making larger modifications (such as abandoning a current intervention and trying something completely new).

◻ **Daily behavior report cards can be used as tracking tools.** Daily behavior report cards are completed by teachers and used to track performance on a daily basis. They are typically used at the Tier II level but can also be used at the Tier III and special education levels. It is ideal to have the daily report card contain items that reflect established schoolwide expectations.

◻ **The RTI model should be evaluated.** By evaluating the RTI model, schools will be better equipped to serve students more effectively and efficiently. Two broad areas to be considered for evaluation are process variables and outcome variables. These variables should be evaluated not only internally by the parties involved directly but also externally by people who may be able to remain more objective with regard to the RTI process in a particular school. In addition to evaluating the process, feedback should be provided to the various RTI teams so that improvements to the system can be made in order to more closely approximate model expectations.

◻ **Parent/guardian involvement and satisfaction are critical.** It is important to keep parents and guardians involved and, at minimum, informed of their child's performance at all levels of the RTI model. In addition, it is equally important to solicit feedback from parents and guardians about their satisfaction with the RTI process. This can often be accomplished in a questionnaire that is provided at the end of problem-solving team meetings and/or at parent–teacher conferences.

REFERENCES

Chafouleas, S. M., McDougal, J. L., Riley-Tillman, T. C., Panahon, C. J., & Hilt, A. M. (2005). What do daily behavior report cards (DBRCs) measure? An initial comparison of DBRCs with direct observation for off-task behavior. *Psychology in the Schools, 42*(6), 669–676.

Chafouleas, S. M., Riley-Tillman, T. C., Sassu, K. A., LaFrance, M. J., & Patwa, S. S. (2007). Daily behavior report cards: An investigation of the consistency of on-task data across raters and methods. *Journal of Positive Behavior Interventions, 9*(1), 30–37.

Cheney, D., Flower, A., & Templeton, T. (2008). Applying Response to Intervention metrics in the social domain for students at risk of developing emotional or behavioral disorders. *Journal of Special Education, 42*(2), 108–126.

Cheney, D. A., Stage, S. A., Hawken, L. S., Lynass, L., Mielenz, C., & Waugh, M. (2009). A 2-year outcome study of the check, connect, and expect intervention for students at risk for severe behavior problems. *Journal of Emotional and Behavioral Disorders, 17*(4), 226–243.

Crone, D., Hawken, L., & Horner, R. (2010). *Responding to problem behavior: The behavior education program* (2nd ed.). New York, NY: Guilford Press.

Fabiano, G. A., Vujnovic, R., Naylor, J., Pariseau, M., & Robins, M. (2009). An investigation of the technical adequacy of a daily behavior report card (DBRC) for monitoring progress of students with attention-deficit/hyperactivity disorder in special education placements. *Assessment for Effective Intervention, 34*(4), 231–241.

Fairbanks, S., Sugai, G., Guardino, D., & Lathrop, M. (2008). Response to Intervention: Examining classroom behavior support in second grade. *Exceptional Children, 73*(3), 288.

Hawken, L. S., MacLeod, K., & Rawlings, L. (2007). Effects of the "behavior education program" (BEP) on office discipline referrals of elementary school students. *Journal of Positive Behavior Interventions, 9*(2), 94–101.

Individuals with Disabilities Education Improvement Act, Pub. L. No. 108–446 (2004).

Johnson-Gros, K., Kaase, K. J., Medley, M. B., Cates, G. L., & Doggett, R. A. (2011). The essential elements matrices: Is RtI a set of interrelated or independent elements? *Journal of Evidence-Based Practices for Schools, 12,* 5–14.

Kazdin, A. (1982). *Single case research designs: Methods for clinical and applied settings.* New York, NY: Oxford University Press.

May, S., Talmadge, N., Todd, A., Horner, R., & Rossetto-Dickey, C. (2009). *Check-in/check-out school-wide information system* (ver. 1.1). Eugene, OR: University of Oregon.

No Child Left Behind Act, Pub. L. No. 107–110 (2001).

Shapiro, E. (2008). Best practices in setting progress monitoring goals for academic skill improvement. In A. Thomas and J. Grimes (Eds.), *Best practices in school psychology V* (pp. 141–158). Bethesda, MD: National Association of School Psychologists.

Walker, B., Cheney, D., Stage, S., Blum, C., & Horner, R. H. (2005). Schoolwide screening and positive behavior supports: Identifying and supporting students at risk for school failure. *Journal of Positive Behavior Interventions, 7*(4), 194–204.

RECOMMENDED RESOURCES

Behavior Reporter: Create Daily and Weekly Behavior Report Cards On-Line (Wright, J.)

www.jimwrightonline.com/php/tbrc/tbrc.php

ChartDog 2.0 (Wright, J.)

www.jimwrightonline.com/php/chartdog_2_0/chartdog.php

Chutes and Ladders Template (Dikowski, B.)

www.measuredeffects.com/index.php?id=23

Illinois Alliance for School-Based Problem Solving and Intervention Resources in Education (I-ASPIRE)

Parent Satisfaction Survey and Other Evaluation Tools

www.luc.edu/cseit/i-aspireresourcesforcoordinator.shtml

Johnston, T. C. (2010). *Data without tears: How to write measureable educational goals and collect meaningful data.* Champaign, IL: Research Press.

Self-Assessment of the Problem-Solving Implementation (SAPSI) and Intervention Fidelity Tool

Loyola University Center for School Evaluation, Intervention, & Training

www.luc.edu/cseit/i-aspireresourcesforcoordinator.shtml

National Center on Student Progress Monitoring

www.studentprogress.org

CHAPTER 5

Effective and Efficient Collaborative Problem-Solving Teams

CHAPTER OVERVIEW

The use of effective and efficient data-based problem solving at the universal (Tier I), targeted (Tier II), and individual student levels (Tier III) is a necessary component of any fully implemented school-based RTI system. Each of these levels may have a problem-solving team charged with making many different decisions not focused exclusively on special education eligibility and entitlement. Integrating and applying RTI concepts discussed in previous chapters with effective systematic problem solving and a multidisciplinary teaming process enables diverse learner needs to be met within an RTI framework—resulting in improved academic and behavioral outcomes for all students. Specifically, this chapter will:

- Provide the purpose and rationale for problem solving.
- Identify common characteristics of problem solving in RTI schools.
- Define collaboration, including its underlying assumptions and importance to effective problem solving.
- Identify the different types of school-based problem-solving teams and how they can be organized within an RTI framework at the building level.
- Identify, discuss the critical components of, and provide examples at the various tiers of the five stages of problem solving (problem identification, problem analysis, plan development, plan implementation, and plan evaluation).
- Identify the characteristics of effective team members.
- Discuss the various roles and responsibilities of team members.
- Discuss various strategies to promote effective group communication and participation.
- Explain how to monitor the implementation of problem solving in your school.

PURPOSE OF AND RATIONALE FOR PROBLEM SOLVING

Problem solving as used in a Response to Intervention model is a process aimed at minimizing or eliminating barriers to success in schools. By utilizing a five-step problem-solving model, school personnel can work more efficiently and effectively with students and each other.

CHARACTERISTICS OF PROBLEM SOLVING

Problem Solving and RTI Are Not the Same

Although, in our experience, many use the terms "problem solving" and "RTI" synonymously, they actually represent two very distinct concepts. Within an RTI framework, problem solving must occur at all three tiers. This problem-solving process not only is similar across tiers, but it is often similar across RTI schools. There are, essentially, four common characteristics of problem solving in effective RTI schools:

◻ First, RTI schools that effectively utilize problem solving are collaborative in nature—that is, effective problem-solving schools often incorporate a team problem-solving approach as opposed to using an expert single-person problem-solver approach.

◻ Second, problem-solving teams adhere to a five-stage process: problem identification, problem analysis, plan development, plan implementation, and plan evaluation.

◻ Third, effective problem-solving schools adopt a standard format with regard to logistics. These logistics include meeting time lines, meeting locations, and delineating roles and responsibilities of team members.

◻ Fourth, RTI schools that effectively implement problem solving focus on evaluating their own effectiveness and problem-solve any barriers that may impede their efficiency and/or effectiveness.

Problem-Solving Teams Are Not Pre-Referral Teams

Problem solving in a generic sense is not new to schools. For example, pre-referral teams have been used in schools for many years. These pre-referral teams are composed of a variety of school professionals including an administrator, classroom teachers, and special service personnel such as the school psychologist or social worker. These are teams that classroom teachers are required to refer students to before initiation of a multidisciplinary evaluation to determine eligibility and entitlement for special education services—hence, the name "pre-referral." Although interventions are frequently developed at these pre-referral team meetings, they are often neither effectively developed (due to limited data) nor consistently implemented.

A major difference between problem-solving teams implemented within an RTI framework and other types of pre-referral intervention teams is the use of a more systematic problem analysis approach and the use of data for decision making (Burns, Wiley, & Viglietta, 2008). It is our experience that the most effective problem-solving teams within an RTI framework use methods associated with the behavioral consultation model (Bergan & Kratochwill, 1990) and focus on techniques of behavioral analysis. These techniques were addressed in greater detail in Chapter 3.

Problem solving utilized within an RTI framework frequently employs collaborative problem-solving concepts and strategies (Fuchs, Fuchs, & Bahr, 1990; Graden, 1989; Graden, Casey, & Bonstrom, 1985; Rosenfield & Gravois, 1996). These concepts and strategies include:

◻ More systematically defining and conceptualizing a problem brought to the team.

◻ Analyzing environmental, curricular, instructional, and individual student factors that influence the problem.

◻ Developing and implementing interventions to address the identified problem.

◻ Monitoring the integrity of the intervention (i.e., the degree to which the intervention is implemented as designed).

◻ Systematically evaluating, through the use of progress monitoring strategies, the effectiveness of the intervention.

These systematic problem-solving components are consistent with the science-based practice of RTI and represent a significant departure from teams referred to in the past as pre-referral.

A COLLABORATIVE APPROACH TO PROBLEM SOLVING

Because the development, implementation, evaluation, and sustaining of RTI requires such a vast amount of professional skill and expertise that no one person in a school is likely to have, we propose that a collaborative approach to problem solving be used. Collaboration can be defined as two or more equal partners working together in a supportive and mutually beneficial relationship. This relationship is voluntary, and the partners share decision making and work toward a common goal (Friend & Cook, 1992). The consultation literature supports a more collaborative approach to decision making (Burns et al., 2008) in terms of effectiveness. Although some researchers in the subject-matter area of consultation are critical of the collaborative approach to consultation and decision making (Erchul, 1999), other research finds that the team-based problem-solving approach contributes to increased student learning, enhances the effectiveness of the team in addressing student concerns, and has a positive effect on systemic variables such as school climate (Idol, Nevin, & Paolucci-Whitcomb, 2000; Burns et al., 2008).

In our experience working with schools implementing RTI, we find that the collaborative teaming/problem-solving process is most effective in making data-based decisions at the various tiers. This is likely because combining the talents, energies, and efforts of a team working collaboratively may yield better results than any one person working in isolation. In addition, we ascribe to the notion that each team member brings to the table unique and varied experiences, perspectives, and expertise, and that each team member has something to contribute to the process.

ORGANIZATION OF A COLLABORATIVE PROBLEM-SOLVING TEAM

Although the purpose of all problem-solving teams is similar, teams may be developed in a variety of ways. Depending on the size of the school (in terms of the number of staff and students), one team may serve all of the functions related to RTI. However, based on our experience, it is more typical to have multiple teams. We will provide examples of the three types of teams corresponding to the three RTI tiers. Keep in mind that these teams may look different depending on the size and level of the school (primary, elementary, secondary). The types of problem-solving teams that we typically encounter at the building level are based on each of the tiers.

Tier I Teams (Building Level)

Organization

Tier I teams, also frequently referred to as building leadership, school improvement, or data analysis teams, focus on problem solving and decision making at the building level.

Membership

It is important that Tier I team membership represents all stakeholders in a building, including the building principal; support staff such as school psychologists, social workers, and speech therapists; special educators; content specialists; and parents and guardians. Administrative support is critical for the success of all problem-solving teams in a school building.

Although it may not be necessary for the building principal to be a member of all teams, it is important that he or she is a member of and actively participates on the Tier I team.

General education teachers from various grade levels who are respected by the staff, along with a representative special education teacher, should also be on the Tier I problem-solving team because teacher empowerment is critical to effective collaborative problem solving and team building. A school psychologist and/or social worker with skills in the collection and interpretation of data and knowledge of the problem-solving/RTI process, as well as a content specialist such as a Title I teacher or literacy coach, should be part of a Tier I team.

Because parent and guardian involvement is a critical aspect of any RTI model (Peterson, Prasse, Shinn, & Swerdlik, 2007), a parent or guardian representative should be included. The team will not be discussing individual student data but rather systemwide data from systemic interventions that were developed through the problem-solving team process; therefore, confidentiality is not an issue. It is important to obtain information from a parent's or guardian's perspective when analyzing systemwide data, considering solutions, and evaluating the effectiveness of systemwide interventions (Peterson et al., 2007).

Responsibilities

Areas considered for problem solving might include resource allocation matters such as:

- ◻ Scheduling personnel.
- ◻ Addressing core curricular issues across grade levels and subject areas, including schoolwide decision making related to selecting curricula.
- ◻ Writing schoolwide behavior plans.
- ◻ Discussing strategies to increase home–school collaboration and parent/guardian involvement.

- ❑ Studying building climate.
- ❑ Matching student needs with instruction and behavior policies and practices.

In addition, Tier I teams analyze schoolwide academic and behavioral data such as the percentage of students meeting benchmarks in particular subject areas, the number of disciplinary infractions for all students during recess or in particular sections of the building, and the total number of student absences at a particular grade level. The team is also involved in determining the effectiveness of Tier I universal instruction as it relates to academic performance and behavior and of Tier I-level targeted interventions delivered through differentiated instruction. Particular grade-level needs may also be discussed based on these data. The Tier I team might also review data on the overall implementation of RTI at the building level, including addressing challenges and monitoring implementation, coordinating training and integrity checks for Tier II standard protocols and Tier III intervention programs, and evaluating the effectiveness of the problem-solving team(s) by reviewing teacher and parent/guardian satisfaction data and various student outcomes.

Tier II Teams (Grade/Path Level)

Organization

Tier II teams, often referred to as grade-level or cluster teams, are often organized around individual grade levels or paths (e.g., a combination of grade levels, such as K–2, depending on the size of the school). In high school, these teams can be grouped by content area (math, science, English, etc.).

Membership

Tier II teams should include a teacher or teachers from each grade level, the school psychologist or a social worker familiar with data collection and analysis procedures, a content specialist or specialists in reading and math, and possibly the school principal.

Responsibilities

Tier II teams often assist the Tier I team in reviewing universal screening data to develop targeted Tier I interventions delivered through differentiated instruction and to identify students in need of additional support through Tier II. This may also include working out the logistics for implementation and monitoring progress of students receiving Tier II interventions. Tier II teams also collaborate with the Tier I teams as needed, such as when choosing standard Tier II interventions.

Tier III Teams (Individual Student)

Organization

Tier III teams, often referred to as student support, student services, or building-level individual problem-solving teams, focus on more intensive, systematic problem solving related to individual student behavior and/or academic issues.

Membership

Tier III teams generally should be composed of four to eight members. These teams often include the principal, the classroom teacher, the student's parents or guardians, and support personnel with relevant expertise in data analysis, accommodations, modifications, and interventions for a wide variety of problems. Teams that do not include school psychologists, speech therapists, social workers, and special educators as permanent members should include these individuals on an as-needed basis. (It should be noted that particular school personnel may be on one or more teams.) In addition, team function and membership can constantly change within a building, based on needs.

Responsibilities

Tier III teams conduct ongoing analysis and interpret progress monitoring data for individual students who have not profited from a combination of universal and Tier II instruction. The team also coordinates individualized interventions, including the logistics of implementation and delivery and assessing the integrity and acceptability of the interventions. The decision making involves identifying interventions for specific problems, which may require an intensity of support that can be provided only through special education. Tier III problem-solving teams are an important part of the special education eligibility process, and the interventions designed and implemented by the team are a key source of data for eligibility decisions.

A summary of the typical organization of teams within a building, including tier levels, typical team names and members, team focus, and associated functions, is provided in Table 5.1.

FIVE STAGES OF THE COLLABORATIVE PROBLEM-SOLVING PROCESS

There are essentially five stages, or phases, to collaborative problem solving:

1. Problem identification
2. Problem analysis
3. Plan development
4. Plan implementation
5. Plan evaluation

We will discuss each phase of the problem-solving model, address major questions, and explain what should occur during each phase. We include examples of what these various stages look like within each of the tier-level teams.

Problem Identification

The first phase of the process is identifying the problem. The goal of this phase is to answer the question, "What is the discrepancy between what is expected (what should be) and what is occurring (what is)?" (Deno, 2002). Five steps are required to answer this question.

TABLE 5. 1   **Summary of the typical organization of teams within a building.**

Tier Level	Typical Team Names	Focus	Associated Functions	Typical Membership
I	Data Team Student Improvement Team Building Leadership Team Core Team	District needs School needs Grade-level needs	Analyze results of universal screening, focusing on building-wide universal curriculum for academic performance and behavior Address buildingwide issues such as school climate and home–school collaboration	Principal Parent/guardian representative School psychologist General education teacher Special education teacher
II	Grade-Level Teams	Class needs Small-group needs	Analyze universal screening results at grade level Select and evaluate effectiveness of Tier II standard protocols Choose students to receive Tier II interventions; render data-based decisions related to continuation, termination, or increasing the intensity of interventions	Grade-level teachers School psychologist Content experts in reading and/or math
III	Individual Problem-Solving Team Student Support Team Intervention Team	Individual student needs	More-intensive problem solving and developing interventions to address academic and/or social-emotional/behavioral concerns that could not be solved at Tier I or II Monitor effectiveness of interventions and make decisions as to continuation, termination, or consideration of special education for individual students	Administrator Classroom teacher and parent or guardian of student being discussed Representative general education teachers Special education teacher Content experts in reading and/or math School psychologist and social worker Others as needed, based on the student being discussed

Step 1: Operationally Define the Problem

The problem should be observable and measureable. Problem-solving teams do not focus, for example, on reducing Attention Deficit Hyperactivity Disorder (ADHD). Instead, they focus on specifics, such as reducing out-of-seat behavior or talking out. The team should not proceed to step 2 unless they can identify the behavior and reliably measure it.

Step 2: Collect Baseline Data

To be successful in the subsequent steps, it is critical that baseline data (i.e., current level of the problem) is identified. In doing so, the team can more effectively prioritize problems;

choose alternative, more functional outcomes; and evaluate the effectiveness of any plan that may be implemented.

Step 3: Prioritize Problems

Each problem behavior should be listed and prioritized in terms of its relative importance. Relative importance is influenced by academic and social expectations (Deno, 2002). For example, for a particular student at the Tier III level, his or her number of friends may not be as important as the goal of decreasing physical aggression and increasing the use of more appropriate expression of anger using words instead of physical means. Once problems are operationally defined and prioritized, it is important to select only one or two problems to target. In doing so, the team can ensure that the appropriate time and resources are being allocated to solving the problem(s) effectively.

Step 4: State the Discrepancy

For the one or two problems selected, the team needs to identify and define a discrepancy between what is expected (based on typical peer performance) and what is occurring. For example, a Tier I team might need to identify the discrepancy between the percentage of students at each grade level who reached benchmarks in reading and the expectation that 80 percent of students at each grade level are meeting benchmarks. A Tier II team may need to identify the discrepancy between the percentage of students receiving Tier II interventions who are not closing the gap with their same-grade peers. A Tier III team might state the discrepancy between the target student's performance and typical peer performance on the universal screening measure for academic performance (USM-A).

Step 5. Identify a Replacement Behavior

Rather than just identifying what the student or groups of students will do (e.g., increase compliance with classroom rules), the focus during problem identification should be on defining a replacement behavior that the team wants the student(s) to engage in and define the behavior in observable concrete terms (e.g., comply with classroom rules 95 percent of the time). It is important not to focus solely on referral problems but rather to identify target replacement behaviors that represent improvements or increases in competencies that the team wants the student(s) to exhibit. Eliminating or reducing problem behaviors does not ensure that desired behaviors will occur—it means that the desired behaviors must be addressed explicitly.

Problem Analysis

The major question to be addressed in the problem-analysis phase of the process is why the problem is occurring. To answer this question, the team should follow the RIOT process discussed in Chapter 3: (1) **r**eview existing data, (2) **i**nterview key personnel involved with the student, (3) **o**bserve the student in relevant environments, and (4) perform additional **t**esting, if necessary.

After completing the RIOT process, the team formulates a hypothesis about the cause of the problem, which likely will be a performance deficiency (won't do) or a skills deficiency (can't do). Academic and social behavior performance deficits often require increasing reinforcement or minimizing punishment for specific behaviors, while skills deficits typically require more systematic instructional intervention.

Plan Development

The two primary questions to answer during plan development, the third phase of problem solving, are what is the goal and how will progress be monitored? Therefore, the major objectives of the plan development phase are to write the goal for the intervention, define the logistics of how the intervention will be implemented, and determine how progress will be monitored. The goal should be written as a measurable statement of expected outcomes (Chapter 4 discusses the goal-setting process in greater detail).

In defining the logistics of the intervention program, the team determines:

◻ What strategies and procedures will be used.

◻ When, where, and how often the intervention will occur.

◻ Who will implement the intervention.

◻ When the intervention will begin and be evaluated (see Chapter 4).

Once these four intervention components are determined, it is important that they be articulated and documented.

Plan Implementation

The fourth phase of problem solving is plan implementation. During this phase, the main question the team addresses is how to ensure integrity of the plan. It is important that the team supports the intervention implementers during this stage. Frequently, as part of this phase, interventions are observed and intervention integrity checklists are completed (see Chapter 4 for a discussion of these and other methods of assessing intervention integrity). Adjustments are made to the plan, if necessary. For example, it might be determined that the intervention time allotment is too long to keep the student's attention. Data should be collected and graphed related to the intervention goal. During this stage, the team should ensure that the plan is being implemented as intended. Therefore, it is suggested that a case manager be assigned and meet with the intervention implementer within two days of the start of a new intervention.

Plan Evaluation

The fifth and final phase of the problem-solving process is plan evaluation. The main question to be answered is "What effect did the plan have on the problem?" To address this question, the team needs to assess whether the student (in Tier II or Tier III) or the whole classroom (in Tier I) is making progress toward the goal established in the plan development stage. Is the student (or the class as a whole) decreasing the behavior identified during the first phase (problem identification)? In addition, determining whether the plan can be maintained in the general education setting is a question often addressed by a Tier III problem-solving team. If it is determined that it cannot be, then a referral for special education eligibility and entitlement is made. These decisions are discussed in more depth in Chapter 4.

CHARACTERISTICS OF EFFECTIVE TEAMS

Effective team members are aware of their value to the team and contribute to a climate of mutual respect, trust, and support. Other characteristics include a commitment to being open and genuine in their communication during team meetings and to the goals of the team. Effective team members believe in a creative problem-solving process and are committed to problem resolution. Team members refrain from "admiring the problem," which occurs when team members spend an excessive amount of time talking about how bad a situation is (such as a student's problems at home) and about factors the team has little or no control over, without focusing on what they *can* control and on how to improve the particular situation. Team members who are willing to put in extra time and effort are a major contributing factor to effective groups. Finally, effective team members are aware of and willing to assume different roles (discussed in the following section) and are always prepared with data to present to the team.

Another important factor to consider about teams is the experience level of individual members. We have observed that recent graduates may be more informed about the problem-solving process used to develop interventions. However, more-experienced team members often possess expert knowledge helpful in data collection and intervention development. We recommend teams comprise a combination of less and more experienced team members.

It is also important not to include as team members personnel who are entrenched in the historic "test and place" forms of problem solving unless they are willing to learn new content and the process of data-based problem solving. These team members must be able to focus on developing effective interventions to address identified problem areas and not solely on determining whether students should be tested for eligibility for special education.

TEAM MEMBERS

Although we identify and discuss some specific roles and responsibilities, it is important to note that all team members are expected to actively participate during the meetings. All members also must assist in collecting data and implementing interventions. They should be knowledgeable and trained in the problem-solving process and related skills. It is not necessary for all team members to personally know the student(s) being discussed, but they should all be committed to the success of the problem-solving process.

There are four people whose presence is important at a problem-solving meeting: the teacher requesting assistance, the principal or other administrator, a specialist in the area of concern, and a parent or guardian of the student. Although others may be included (such as a special education teacher, school psychologist, school social worker, speech/language pathologist, and/or occupational therapist), they are not required and can be present on an as-needed basis.

Teacher Requesting Assistance

The teacher requesting assistance attends all meetings and helps collect data. This teacher is also frequently involved in implementing the intervention. He or she is responsible for communicating with the parents or guardians of the student who is the subject of the problem-solving meeting and should invite them to meetings (unless this is done by the case manager). It is critical that the teacher feel supported because he or she conducts the majority of work in Tier III problem solving at the intervention implementation stages (Peterson et al., 2007). This teacher may require support and training to implement all of the interventions and to monitor their effectiveness. In addition to implementing specific interventions, the teacher may be asked to make adaptations or changes to the classroom environment as part of the problem-solving process. It is important that this teacher understands the problem-solving process and does not play another role during the meeting.

Principal or Other Administrator

The principal or another administrator ensures that the problem-solving process in the building is implemented effectively. He or she must be supportive of the process and allocate the necessary resources, such as time and a comfortable place to meet. The administrator also monitors staff climate and communicates the importance of the problem-solving process to all staff and parents/guardians. Further, the administrator communicates clearly that the use of the problem-solving process by a teacher or group of teachers is not indicative of teacher weakness but of teacher competence and that interventions need to be implemented with integrity before special education is considered.

Parent or Guardian

The parent or guardian typically knows his or her child best and represents a critical member of the problem-solving team. He or she can contribute at all stages of the problem-solving process, including problem identification, problem analysis, plan development, and implementation. Effective home–school collaboration has a strong relationship to academic achievement (Esler, Godber, & Christenson, 2008). Also, our experience is that the more parents and guardians perceive that they are involved in the process, the more satisfied they are with problem solving and the more likely to view the school positively (Peterson et al., 2007).

Specialists

Other professionals can be invited to problem-solving meetings based on the needs of the student and the nature of the problem behaviors (academic, social-emotional, and/or behavioral) being addressed. These professionals can include the school psychologist, social worker, speech and language therapist, occupational and/or physical therapist, special education teacher, and reading or math specialist.

TEAM MEMBER RESPONSIBILITIES

We have found that effective teams have specific roles and responsibilities for their members. Some of the roles are unique to the level or tier of problem solving. Although certain team roles, such as facilitator or process specialist, might be permanently assigned, others are intended to rotate. Because not everyone is capable of performing all roles effectively, we do not recommend that roles be randomly rotated. (Note: It is important that none of these roles be assigned to anyone identified in the previous section who is not a permanent member of the team, such as the parent or guardian or the teacher requesting assistance.)

The following are roles that we have commonly observed during problem-solving team meetings: facilitator, timekeeper, jargon buster, justifier, process specialist, parent/guardian advocate, note taker, and case (data) manager.

Facilitator

One of the most critical roles is that of the facilitator. A goal of the facilitator is to encourage active participation of all team members. We have observed that school psychologists and special educators typically provide a disproportionately larger input compared to other team members—with classroom teachers and parents/guardians being less active participants. These differences in participation rates can have implications for the degree of satisfaction with team decisions and "buy-in" for intervention plans. It is necessary, therefore, that the facilitator keep everyone involved. Making sure that team members have explicit knowledge about roles and expectations during the problem-solving process can help accomplish this goal.

The facilitator should structure communication so that all members contribute in an organized manner. For example, he or she might ask teachers and parents/guardians to contribute first and provide them with appropriate prompts and supports. Other team members can be called on to contribute after the teacher and parents/guardians have had their chance.

The facilitator also ensures the integrity of the problem-solving process and supports effective communication. Major tasks are to keep the team on track, to make sure that the steps of problem solving are followed during the meeting, and to promote effective group communication and participation. Effective facilitators are knowledgeable about the problem-solving process, have group-process skills, are assertive, and are strong leaders. Not everyone will be a successful facilitator.

To accomplish these communication goals, facilitators use active listening skills:

◻ To help clarify statements:

"Tell me more about that ..."

"Then what happened?"

◻ To affirm statements, feelings, attitudes, and opinions:

"It seems that you feel ..."

"It sounds like you are concerned about how much time it may take to get this intervention started in your classroom. What can we do to assist you with getting started?"

- ▫ To encourage participants:

    "When we develop your strategy, please tell us more about your experiences with this approach."

- ▫ To summarize information:

    "Let's make sure I understand everything …"

    "We have now identified a discrepancy between what is expected and what is occurring as part of the problem identification stage. Now let's develop some hypotheses about why that problem is occurring as we move into the problem analysis step of problem solving. "

    "Do we all agree that the hypothesis we developed is that Craig is reading only ten words per minute because he lacks phonological awareness?"

- ▫ To explore and clarify implications:

    "What do you think this means?"

    "What do you think about that?"

    "How do you think this will affect …"?

To ensure timely completion of the various steps of problem solving, facilitators encourage brief and concise comments. To do this, a facilitator should:

- ▫ Ask team members to share only the most important information.
- ▫ Share patterns of behavior (such as during which classes or subjects the behavior tends to occur and what typically follows the behavior, such as peer or teacher attention).
- ▫ Summarize raw data.
- ▫ Refrain from providing additional information if there are no further concerns.
- ▫ Allow time for questions and clarification.

Some facilitators use posters or flip charts showing the stages of problem solving and the principles of effective communication. These visual aids serve as guides and reminders for the entire team.

Finally, the following are some effective group management/process strategies that can be employed by the facilitator.

Communicating Purpose

It is important that members know the purpose of each meeting and be made aware of the amount of time scheduled. The facilitator might begin the meeting by saying, "We have 40 minutes to go through the problem-solving process, so let's begin."

Managing Conflict

The facilitator helps the team come to a consensus. Consensus can be defined as a decision that is not necessarily everyone's first choice but is one that everyone can live with. A facilitator might say something like this: "From what I am hearing, we have developed more than one intervention strategy that may meet Gary's needs. Mrs. Blum [classroom teacher], of the two options, do you have a sense of what may work better in your classroom?" or

"Can we agree to try this intervention that Mrs. Smith believes will work better in her class-room, and we'll use our progress monitoring data to determine the effectiveness of that intervention when we get back together in two weeks?"

Staying on Task

It is important that the facilitator assist the team in staying on task while working through the different stages of problem solving. The facilitator must ensure that all team members know what step of the problem-solving process they are in at all times, that the information is summarized, and that an effort is made to reach consensus.

Timekeeper

A timekeeper helps the team stay on track by enforcing time limits for meetings and keeping the team aware of the time. In our experience, time factors are the most frequently cited concern for problem-solving teams at all tiers. Challenges include finding convenient meeting times, meetings that take too much time, and lack of time to accomplish all that is necessary in a problem-solving meeting. Further, we have found that team decision making is adversely affected by unrealistic time constraints and that the quality of decisions is negatively affected by the need to rush to decisions in order to stay on schedule. The timekeeper must be assertive and may play other roles as well. The amount of time needed for actual team meetings can be reduced if certain tasks are accomplished before the meeting (e.g., an interview conducted by the case manager with the teacher to define specific problem behaviors that are then shared by the teacher at the team meeting). The actual meeting should last no more than 20 to 30 minutes at Tier III (Burns et al., 2008).

Jargon Buster

The use of jargon or unfamiliar terminology often interferes with effective problem solving. The jargon buster listens for terminology that may be unfamiliar to any team members, including the parent or guardian. After the jargon buster points out an unfamiliar term, the person who used the term is asked to define it.

Justifier

The justifier asks team members to explain why they made a particular conclusion. This role is particularly important during the stages of problem analysis (when various hypotheses are being explored) and plan development. It is also important for team members to understand why representatives of particular disciplines chose various assessment methods or made inferences based on their assessment data. Collaborative problem solving is facilitated when rationales are provided for various conclusions or inferences.

Process Specialist

The process specialist provides the team with feedback on how they work together as a team and engage in effective problem solving. The process specialist helps teams work more effectively in collaborative problem solving. He or she comments on such factors as the extent of participation across disciplines, whether team members have been heard and respected, and the ease and effectiveness of moving through the various stages of problem solving.

Parent/Guardian Advocate

A parent/guardian advocate is not a role that we typically see assigned, but it is a potentially very valuable one. It is assigned to a school staff member who ensures that parent or guardian involvement occurs. He or she also monitors the parent's or guardian's reaction to what occurs during the meeting and ensures that the parent or guardian's rights are upheld. The advocate may also be the person who (1) makes initial contact with the parent or guardian to say that a problem-solving meeting is scheduled, (2) interviews the parent or guardian before the meeting, (3) answers any questions before and after the meeting that the parent or guardian may have, and (4) tries to make the parent or guardian feel as comfortable as possible.

Note Taker

The note taker is responsible for documenting the meeting. The note taker should also summarize information when necessary and notify the team when a problem-solving stage has been omitted. Characteristics of an effective note taker include being detail oriented, staying on task, and knowing the five steps of the problem-solving process. We suggest that the note taker use technology to make meeting notes easily available (such as posting them on the school listserv with, of course, appropriate cautions about confidentiality of information about particular pupils). Forms should be used to facilitate note taking.

Case Manager

In Tier III problem-solving meetings, a case (data) manager may be assigned to facilitate the student's case and serve as the contact person. It is critical that this individual be competent in problem identification, problem analysis, and collaboration. The case manager is responsible for communicating with parents or guardians and teachers and ensuring that the required data are collected and summarized at the meetings, as well as determining that the intervention is being implemented as intended. It is helpful for teams to have written guidelines for serving as a case manager and to rotate this role among various team members based on their skills and interests. A case manager can also help the team stay within established time limits so that they can spend more time defining and analyzing the problem and developing a plan. The case manager should be appointed before the first problem-solving meeting. The person assuming this role documents the reason for which the child has been referred for problem solving, reviews records, assists the referring teacher in bringing helpful information to the meeting, and assists in interviewing parents. Characteristics of effective case managers include being organized and having strong interpersonal and communication skills.

TEAM MEETING LOGISTICS AND TIME LINES

It is our experience that the most successful teams have a designated meeting space that is comfortable and has adequate space for teamwork. Team members should have easy access to confidential student files during team meetings. If these practices are established as routine, meeting time is used efficiently. Likewise, effective teams strive to complete any tasks that can be done another time in order to ensure that team meeting time is reserved for the purpose of collaborative problem solving.

Most Tier III teams meet on a weekly basis, but meeting frequency depends on the size of the school and the number of referrals. For Tier III meetings, each case should take between 20 and 30 minutes. Tier III teams should meet within 1 or 2 weeks after a request for assistance has been received from a teacher. This time line gives the team time to collect data to assist with problem identification and analysis. A team member should also meet with the intervention implementer(s) within the first two days of intervention for implementation and then follow up weekly for the next several weeks. Follow-up meetings should be scheduled at the initial problem-solving meeting and be based on individual student case and progress monitoring data, which should be collected weekly.

A Tier I team should meet at least three times per year after universal screening data have been collected, or more often, depending on building-level issues that need to be addressed. Tier II (grade-level) teams, should meet monthly or bi-monthly.

SUMMARY OF IMPORTANT POINTS

- ◻ **Pre-referral teams are not the same as collaborative problem-solving teams.** Problem-solving teams employ a systematic, collaborative approach and rely on data for decision making.

- ◻ **Problem solving within an RTI framework must occur at all three tiers.** Although the focus and team membership may differ, effective RTI implementation includes systematic, collaborative problem solving at all three tiers.

- ◻ **Teams at different tiers have different foci.** Tier I teams focus on buildingwide issues such as the effectiveness of universal curriculum/instructional practices and school climate. Tier II teams are organized based on individual grade levels and focus on choosing targeted Tier II interventions, deciding which students should receive interventions, and evaluating the effectiveness of individual interventions. Tier III teams spend their time on more-intensive, individualized problem solving.

- ◻ **Teams at different tiers have different types of members.** Tier I teams should include all stakeholders as members. Tier II teams, organized around grade levels, include classroom teachers as members. Tier III teams include four to eight individuals with expertise in data analysis, accommodations, modifications, and interventions for a wide variety of problems.

- ◻ **Collaboration is an important characteristic of problem solving within an RTI framework.** Collaboration is a mutually beneficial and supportive relationship among all members, who share in decision making and work toward a common goal.

- ◻ **Systematic, collaborative problem solving consists of five stages.** These stages are problem identification, problem analysis, plan development, plan implementation, and plan evaluation. *Problem identification* answers the question, "What is the discrepancy between what is expected and what is occurring?" *Problem analysis* asks, "Why is the problem occurring?" *Plan development* addresses the question, "What is the plan and the goal and how will the progress be monitored?" *Plan implementation* addresses ways in which integrity of the plan can be ensured. *Plan evaluation* explores how well the plan addressed the problem.

□ **Effective team members have certain characteristics.** Some of these characteristics include commitment to problem resolution, commitment to being open and genuine in communication, and being creative problem solvers. On effective teams, all members have a responsibility for being knowledgeable and trained in systematic problem solving and being dedicated to the success of the problem-solving process. In addition, team members—including the teacher requesting assistance, the principal/administrator, specialist(s) in area of concern, and the parent or guardian—play unique roles and have specific responsibilities. Finally, effective problem solving and teaming require balanced participation by all team members.

□ **Effective teams have a number of rotating roles.** These roles include facilitator, timekeeper, jargon buster, justifier, process specialist, parent/guardian advocate, note taker, and case (data) manager.

□ **Consistent and effective use of time are essential.** Meeting at a consistent time and in the same place and never accomplishing at a meeting what can be done at another time are also characteristics of effective teams. For maximum efficiency, Tier III teams should meet for no longer than 30 minutes per student. Most Tier III teams meet weekly, while Tier I teams should meet on a regular basis—at least three times per year but possibly more often if there are building-level issues that need to be addressed. Tier II teams should meet monthly or bi-monthly. In a particular school, the frequency of meetings depends on team tier level, size of the school building, and number of referrals for problem solving at each tier.

□ **It is important to respond quickly to teacher requests for assistance.** Tier III teams should meet no more than two weeks after a referral by a teacher.

REFERENCES

Bergan, J. R., & Kratochwill, T. R. (1990). *Behavioral consultation and therapy.* New York, NY: Plenum.

Burns, M. K., Wiley, H. I., & Viglietta, E. (2008). Best practices in facilitating problem-solving teams. In A. Thomas and J. Grimes (Eds.), *Best practices in school psychology V* (pp. 1633–1644). Bethesda, MD: National Association of School Psychologists.

Deno, S. L. (2002). Problem solving as "best practice." In A. Thomas & J. Grimes (Eds.), *Best practices in school psychology IV* (pp. 37–66). Bethesda, MD: National Association of School Psychologists.

Erchul, W. P. (1999). Two steps forward, one step back: Collaboration in school-based consultation. *Journal of School Psychology, 37,* 191–203.

Esler, A. N., Godber, Y., & Christenson, S. L. (2008). Best practices in supporting school–family partnerships. In A. Thomas and J. Grimes (Eds.), *Best practices in school psychology V* (pp. 917–936). Bethesda, MD: National Association of School Psychologists.

Friend, M., & Cook, L. (1992). *Interactions: Collaboration skills for school professionals.* White Plains, NY: Longman.

Fuchs, D., Fuchs, L. S., & Bahr, M. W. (1990). Mainstream assistance teams: A scientific basis for the art of consultation. *Exceptional Children, 57,* 128–139.

Graden, J. L. (1989). Reactions to school consultation: Some considerations from a problem-solving perspective. *Professional School Psychology, 4,* 29–35.

Graden, J. L., Casey, C., & Bonstrom, O. (1985). Implementing a prereferral intervention system: II, The data. *Exceptional Children, 51,* 487–496.

Idol, L., Nevin, A., & Paolucci-Whitcomb, O. (2000). *Collaborative consultation* (3rd ed.). Austin, TX: PRO-ED.

Peterson, D. L., Prasse, D., Shinn, M., & Swerdlik, M. E. (2007). The Illinois flexible service delivery model: A problem-solving model initiative. In S.R. Jimerson, M. K. Burns, and A. VanDerHeyden (Eds.), *The handbook of response to intervention: The science and practice of assessment and intervention.* New York, NY: Springer Science.

Rosenfield, S. A., & Gravois, T. A. (1996). *Instructional consultation teams: Collaborating for change.* New York, NY: Guilford Press.

ADDITIONAL SOURCES

Allen, S. J., & Graden, J. L. (2002). Best practices in collaborative problem-solving for intervention design. In A. Thomas and J. Grimes (Eds.), *Best practices in school psychology IV* (pp. 565–582). Bethesda, MD: National Association of School Psychologists.

Batsche, G., Castillo, J., Dixon, D. N., & Forde, S. (2008). Linking assessment to intervention. In A. Thomas and J. Grimes (Eds.), *Best practices in school psychology V* (pp. 177–194). Bethesda, MD: National Association of School Psychologists.

Burns, G. (1995). The secrets of team facilitation. *Training and Development 49*(6), 46–52. www.pathwise.com/library/secrets_of_team_facilitation.pdf

Iverson, A. (2002). Best practices in problem-solving team structure and process. In A. Thomas and J. Grimes (Eds.), *Best practices in school psychology IV* (pp. 657–670). Bethesda, MD: National Association of School Psychologists.

Raforth, M. A., & Foriska, T. (2006). Administrator participation in promoting effective problem-solving teams. *Remedial and Special Education (27)* 3, 130–135.

RECOMMENDED RESOURCES

Problem Solving and Response to Intervention Evaluation Tools

http://www.floridarti.usf.edu/resources/program_evaluation/evaluation_tools/index.html

Illinois Alliance for School-Based Problem-Solving and Intervention Resources in Education (I-ASPIRE)

Resources for Program Coordinators

www.luc.edu/cseit/i-aspireresourcesforcoordinator.shtml

CHAPTER 6

Special Topics in RTI

CHAPTER OVERVIEW

RTI is a relatively new concept in schools, and many questions related to its implementation often present themselves unexpectedly. This chapter aids in the understanding of the implementation of RTI as it relates to topics not commonly addressed in the literature and often overlooked in practice. In general, this chapter seeks to provide insight to school personnel in dealing with these special topics. In addition, this chapter builds on and supports the objectives of previous chapters. Specifically, this chapter will:

- ▫ Explain the role of special education in the RTI model.
- ▫ Discuss what is meant by a continuum of supports.
- ▫ Discuss how to use a comprehensive data system.
- ▫ Show how data can be used to decide whether a student can exit special education.
- ▫ Demonstrate how different types of behavioral data can be incorporated into the decision-making process.
- ▫ Explain what assistive technology is and how it can be monitored using the RTI model.
- ▫ Describe the role of treatment integrity and a basic method of measurement.
- ▫ Show how RTI can be used effectively for culturally or linguistically diverse learners.
- ▫ Describe universal design for learning and how it can be integrated into a comprehensive RTI model.
- ▫ Discuss how comprehensive RTI could be implemented at the secondary level.
- ▫ Discuss how to select evidence-based practices.

ROLE OF THE SPECIAL EDUCATOR AND AVOIDING THE PITFALLS OF CHANGE

Throughout this book, we emphasize the use of data-based decision making as critical to the success of implementing RTI in a school. Our discussion about RTI centers on the important role of general educators within this new framework and their roles in a systematic problem-solving process. However, special educators and existing special education programs have important educational roles to play in all aspects of the RTI process. These roles include working with children in special education as well as at-risk students.

Working directly with students who are at risk represents a new role for special educators. Traditionally, special education has focused on service delivery, program development, and data-based decision making for students identified for special education services only. As discussed in the first chapter of this book, this approach produced a "wait-to-fail" model of service delivery. This has not been effective, and, in some school districts, it has resulted in large percentages of students, particularly students of color, receiving special education services more frequently.

In the United States, when systems changes are proposed to improve educational outcomes, they are often implemented without strong research support, and successful practices are often replaced in order to make room for the "reformed system" (Fullan, 2007). This happens so frequently in American schools that educators tend say to themselves, "Here we go again." In the U.S. educational system, this is often referred to as "throwing the baby out with the bathwater."

We therefore suggest that you not approach change in special education as it relates to RTI in this way. We believe that there are many effective practices that special and general educators already engage in that support a comprehensive RTI approach. That said, we have found that using special educators in new, efficient, and effective ways may better support implementation in a comprehensive RTI model.

Since passage in 1975 of the Education for All Handicapped Children's Act (Pub. L. No. 94–142), educators have struggled with how best to serve students with disabilities. Initially, many school districts believed it was best to maintain special schools or classrooms for most students with disabilities. Then there was a widespread initiative to include, or "mainstream," students with special needs—even those with severe disabilities—into the general education classroom. In this model of service delivery, students with special needs are educated alongside their peers. Accommodations and modifications are implemented by the general educator, in collaboration or while co-teaching with a special educator. Sometimes, if the support is needed, a special education paraprofessional is provided. Both of these models have been implemented with some degree of success. In most school districts today, you can find a continuum of services available to students with special needs. This continuum of services is a legal requirement, and it helps support students with many different types of needs. Additionally, other aspects of the special education law, such as transition, functional behavior assessment, and assistive technology, are being implemented in schools across the United States and producing positive outcomes for children with disabilities. Although increased access to an appropriate education and increased positive outcomes are positive contributions to our current special education system, most educators are not satisfied with the uneven results (Brownell, Sindelar, Kiely, & Danielson, 2010; Wagner, Newman, Cameto, & Levine, 2006).

THE SPECIAL EDUCATOR AND RTI

We believe that more-direct measures of academic performance and social-emotional behaviors can more effectively lead to interventions that improve the quality of special education services than traditional assessment and "wait-to-fail" models. This point is particularly important to the special educator, who is at the heart of intervention delivery to students with disabilities. Although traditional special education methods such as developing accommodations, making modifications, or providing compensatory support for a student with a disability will always be an essential part of the special educator's job, RTI increases the emphasis on special educators serving the role of interventionist. Although the role of the interventionist is not completely foreign to most special educators, in comprehensive RTI models, that role is essential to achieving success.

What Does It Mean to Be an Interventionist?

As noted, special educators make accommodations or modifications such that students with disabilities can gain appropriate access to the curriculum. For students with severe intellectual disabilities or physical disabilities, this is an appropriate educational approach. These students need special accommodations or modifications to increase curriculum accessibility and meaningfulness. In some instances, an alternative life skills curriculum is essential. However, for students with any disability—even those with a severe intellectual disability—*overaccommodation* can lead to dependency and can unintentionally foster disabling behaviors.

Although access will always remain important, one implication of a comprehensive RTI model is that the special educator needs to do more than simply develop accommodations and modifications to help students with disabilities gain access to the curriculum. Specifically, the special educator needs to be an active intervention agent to help students acquire, maintain, generalize, and adapt both academic and social behavior skills. The comprehensive RTI model is founded on the principle that if we collect meaningful data, we can then intervene to prevent learning difficulties from becoming more pervasive and enable educators to improve student performance through intervention based on these data. Therefore, it is essential that special educators monitor progress systematically and apply specially designed instruction with the goal of improving a student's performance.

Historically, special educators have infrequently found effective methods for exiting students from special education (U.S. Department of Education, 2006). More often, teachers and their school administrators pursued means of support to increase student success in special education, often in more restrictive and isolated environments. Although many students with disabilities need special education services for their entire education, focusing on decreasing dual discrepancy (as discussed in Chapter 2) will likely facilitate the exit of many students from special education. For students whose performance discrepancies do not support exiting them from the system, the direct assessment and intervention perspective of RTI will likely result in better outcomes.

UNDERSTANDING THE CONTINUUM OF SUPPORTS

By default, all students in special education need some level of support (Figure 6.1). These supports are multifaceted, are multicomponent (i.e., they consist of multiple parts that serve a critical purpose as a whole), and some cut across multiple educational domains (math, reading, social behavior, etc.). For a student to exit special education, he or she must be able to demonstrate progress in the general education environment with a minimal amount of support. Although we advocate a shift away from a modification and accommodation model to an interventionist model, we assume that special education accommodation, modifications, and compensatory supports through assistive technology will be in place for students who have an IEP.

FIGURE 6.1   **Continuum of intensity of supports.**

High-intensity supports (e.g., behavior support plans, modifying the curriculum)

Low-intensity supports (e.g., prompts, extra time on tests)

In a comprehensive RTI model, the goal of the special educator is to reduce the performance discrepancy between the special education student and his or her peers, or between the special education student and a criterion, in order to provide an appropriate education in the least restrictive environment. One of the complex tasks is not only to monitor dual discrepancy but also to track level of support along with educational progress. A special educator must be equipped to deal with students requiring different levels of support, having different rates of progress, and performing at different skill levels. As shown in Figure 6.2, Craig is making progress toward grade level. In fact, his rate of progress is stronger than that of typical peers, although still below grade level. However, substantial supports are needed to maintain that progress. It is unlikely that this student could benefit solely from a general education level of support. Instead, these accommodations and modifications may need to be monitored by the special educator such that fading or intensifying is implemented as needed.

DEVELOPING A COMPREHENSIVE DATA SYSTEM FOR SPECIAL EDUCATION

Special educators should be competent and proficient in the use of all data collection methods discussed in previous chapters. However, with regard to special education specifically, there are some unique practices that also should be commonly utilized. First, the frequency of data collection needs to be increased for students receiving special education services. We recommend a minimum of biweekly, but, in some cases, as frequently as twice per week might be necessary. Just like students across all tiers of service in an RTI model, the progress of students with special education needs should be monitored frequently so that educators can make necessary adjustments in any interventions those students are being provided.

A second common practice of special education is linking IEP goals to the procedures for monitoring progress. In addition to IEP teams developing meaningful goals for each student, special educators must ensure that reliable and valid methods for monitoring progress, such as curriculum-based measurements (CBMs), align with the IEP goals. It is

FIGURE 6.2   **Example of monitoring student progress, by a special educator.**

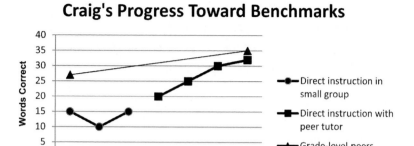

important, however, to note that not all CBMs track all aspects of an IEP goal or benchmark. For example, consider the following IEP goal:

> Given one verbal prompt to focus her attention, Jennifer will read aloud randomly selected third-grade-level passages with 85 words correct per minute for three consecutive CBM probes by May 15, as measured by data collected by the educational staff.

All of those components of the IEP goal can be monitored on a graph and the CBM data sheet except the underlying condition of low level of attention. However, it should be noted that by using a separate graph and additional data collection procedures (e.g., systematic, direct behavior observation recording), attention can also be operationally defined and monitored. It is not unusual for a special educator to incorporate this type of support into a goal to help students achieve success in a comprehensive RTI approach. In this case, the IEP team has hypothesized that Jennifer needs an extra prompt to help her focus on the task. In fact, Jennifer may need multiple prompts, but the IEP team would like her to need only one. Depending on the circumstances, there are many conditions that may be incorporated into an objective or annual goal that may not be directly accounted for by CBM (extra time, wait time, visual cues, etc.). Several data collection strategies can help special educators in a comprehensive RTI assessment model collect and monitor data of conditions that are not built into a CBM. Examples of several data collection strategies follow:

▫ Write the "on the condition" on the CBM data collection sheet (e.g., make a note of the prompt).

▫ Create an informal data sheet to complement the CBM data collection sheet.

▫ Graph changes in conditions alongside student progress.

▫ Use phase lines (a line on the graph marking where the change took place) to mark significant changes, as shown in Figure 6.2.

▫ Note small adjustments with an arrow (see Chapter 3).

See *Data Without Tears* (Johnston, 2010) for a more in-depth discussion on writing measurable goals and utilizing data within an RTI framework in special education.

TRACKING ALL DOMAINS OF NEED: A COMPREHENSIVE APPROACH

Special educators and the families of students with disabilities are aware that many students have multiple needs. Broad areas of needs are often referred to as educational domains. For example, writing, mathematics, reading, and social behavior are four core domains of instruction for which a student with a disability may require specially designed instruction. In Chapter 3, we discussed extensively how to use CBM in each of the academic domains. These data collection methods should also be implemented with special education students. As mentioned previously, CBM data collection for a student in special education needs to be frequent. Doing so creates a comprehensive assessment of the student with special needs and helps ensure that the educational team is providing effective instruction.

Not all students with special needs have goals and objectives in every educational domain. However, in a comprehensive model of RTI, student progress should be monitored in all domains, regardless of IEP goals and objectives. For example, Jamal is a student with a learning disability whose primary areas of educational need are reading and writing. Jamal is provided with specially designed instruction in those two areas 60 minutes per day by a special education teacher. CBM data are collected, and Jamal's educational progress is monitored closely by the special educator.

However, consider two other important characteristics of Jamal's performance. First, Jamal is at grade level in mathematics. Second, he continues to exhibit minor behavioral problems but not at a level that would identify him as a student with emotional or behavior disorders. These behavior problems may indicate mild social skills deficits. In a comprehensive model of RTI, Jamal's progress might be monitored with intensive CBM of reading and writing administered by the special education teacher, ongoing monitoring of progress in mathematics administered in the general education classroom, and daily monitoring for schoolwide behavioral expectations by both the special education and general education teachers.

This is a significant departure from past assessment practices. In a comprehensive RTI model, assessment of student performance in special education is more focused and frequent than a once per year review of IEP goals or standardized test results. Figure 6.3 lists several characteristics in a comprehensive RTI model that are significantly different from traditional models of special education assessment. For example, in a comprehensive RTI model, assessment varies in frequency and may be administered by different individuals depending on the needs of the student. In our example, Jamal receives intensive CBM by the special educator, which includes daily monitoring of progress; takes part in a social skills training program designed for early intervention prior to special education; and is monitored in mathematics at a level typical for that of his peers. For Jamal, many types of educators are part of the assessment process, and he may be participating in educational programs that are not delivered by the special education teacher.

USING COMPREHENSIVE ASSESSMENT TO AVOID THE SLIDING EFFECT

A student identified for special education services in one domain (e.g., reading or math) might continue to develop more learning difficulties over time. In a comprehensive RTI model, instructional supports, as well as assessment, are delivered on a continuum to match the needs of each student. This principle is critical because failure to monitor special educa-

FIGURE 6.3   Comprehensive RTI versus traditional models of special education assessment.

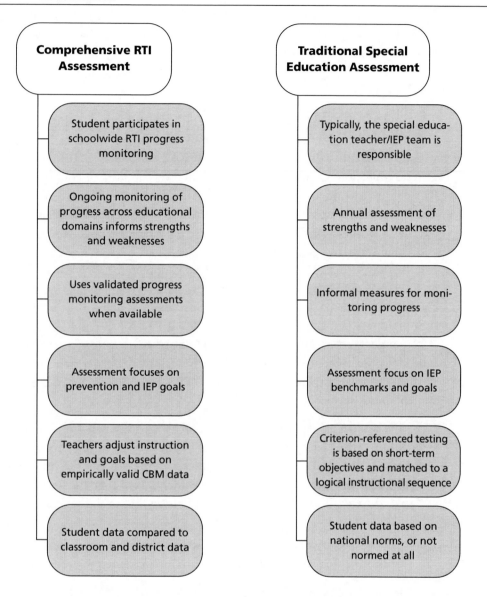

tion students via a comprehensive model can result in a sliding effect—that is, in a traditional model of special education assessment, students have to wait until their performances have slid far enough behind that of their grade-level peers to receive services. For example, a student may initially be identified as having reading difficulties; as a result, the pupil receives resource support to address those needs as identified in the IEP. However, the student may also need assistance in mathematics but is not so far behind that he or she qualifies for special education services in that domain. In a traditional model, which does not address these potential deficits through proactive, early intervention, the student slides into more significant discrepancies across multiple educational domains before he or she can gain services. Using a comprehensive RTI model of assessment, a student who might not qualify for special education services, but who may be at risk, can be identified early and receive targeted intervention.

The state of Illinois has mandated the use of RTI for the identification of special education needs. We mention this because the Illinois State Board of Education (ISBE, 2010a, 2010b) provides guidelines and answers to frequently asked questions that are very helpful in navigating through the eligibility determination process. These documents also prove helpful in understanding the process for exiting special education.

EXITING SPECIAL EDUCATION

The comprehensive approach to RTI may afford some students the opportunity to exit special education. We do not support the discontinuation of special education services without substantive evidence that a student's performance is adequately improving in general education without special education–level supports. A comprehensive model of RTI will not eliminate the need for special education, and we absolutely believe that students who need special education services and supports should receive them. For most educators, this requires the systematic use of data to determine whether the provision of additional support services is warranted.

Because exiting a student from special education prematurely can have painful consequences for a student, it is important that this decision be made cautiously, systematically, and based on data that predict success. All decisions need to be made by the IEP team, and the opinions of family members (as part of the IEP team) should be given special weight. When students are mature enough, they should also participate in this important decision. It is critical that no one individual or administrator alone determines that a student exit special education. A guiding question for IEP teams to consider in the evaluation of a student to exit special education is this:

1. Is the student able to learn at the rate and level without all of the supports of special education for at least a 6-week period? (In this situation, minor accommodations and specially designed instruction are available to the student, but modifications of the curriculum should not be made for the student.) If so, then the student can be considered for removal of supports as a trial. During that trial, the team should answer a second question.

2. Can the student continue that progress for another 8-week period in the general education setting with no special accommodations, interventions, or supports?

The premise behind this logic is that before a student can even be considered for a trial without support, he or she must be able to make progress at the level of typical peers with only a minimal amount of special education assistance. If the answer to the first question is yes, then the special education team can safely consider a trial with a reasonable chance of success. Asking the first question and providing a data-based answer reduce the chances that the IEP team has incorrectly identified a student as being ready for exit. If the answer to the second question is yes, *and* if the IEP team agrees it is appropriate, exiting special education is worth consideration.

It should be assumed that accommodations will not continue when a student is placed in general education. Even in comprehensive RTI schools, where more supports for at-risk students are available, those supports cannot be compared to the intensity of specially designed instruction and supports available to a student in special education. IEP teams need to proceed with caution and ensure that the student is capable of learning without individualized instruction and supports. We do not recommend that any student be exited from special education before undergoing a trial period in general education during which data are collected to answer the second question.

If a student is not able to make adequate progress, the law permits the student to remain in general education with specially designed supports if it is the least restrictive educational environment (IDEIA, 2004). Because of the risk of a student losing important learning time, it is essential that progress be monitored intensively during a trial in general education to determine whether he or she is able to perform academically and/or socially with only general education instruction. If the IEP team notices during a trial period that the student's academic performance and/or behavior begins to decline after 2 to 3 weeks, it is best that the trial be terminated and the student continue to receive specially designed interventions and supports. The student is not ready for exit from special education at that point in his or her education.

SOCIAL BEHAVIOR COMPETENCY IN SPECIAL EDUCATION

Functional Behavior Assessment

Many students in special education also have behavior problems. Some of these students may have social skills deficits, while others may have more complex mental health problems. For many of these students, a functional behavior assessment (FBA) or functional analysis (FA) is an appropriate assessment. Chapter 3 provides a general overview of FBA and FA. Although the FBA can be helpful at the Tier III and special education levels of support, we often suggest that a full FA be conducted at the special education level.

Incorporating Social Behavior Data

In any classroom there are students who perform along a continuum that mirrors the larger RTI continuum described in Chapter 1. Social competency is no exception. A special education teacher may have students who present no behavior problems, some that present minimal but problematic behavior problems, and others who have extremely intensive behavior problems who need functional behavior assessment and a positive behavior support plan developed for them. Special education teachers should use the same progress monitoring and screening assessments previously discussed in this book.

Academic Engaged Time

One gross indicator of social competency is academic engaged time (AET). For a student to be engaged, he or she must be able to follow directions, ask for help, ignore distractions, self-regulate, and demonstrate impulse control. Students who cannot perform these behaviors often are distractible, have difficulty engaging in content, and can be very disruptive in the classroom. These types of problems are often related to social skills deficits. Not surprisingly, there exists a strong relationship between AET and academic performance (e.g., Heward 2003; Miller, Gunter, Venn, Hummel, & Wiley, 2003). For example, we would not expect a student who was on task 20 percent of the time during math to perform as well on a math test as a student who is on task 80 percent of the time. However, we cannot assume that just because the student is engaging academically that he or she is learning. For students who are not making academic or behavioral growth, it can be important to chart AET on their academic performance graph (Figure 6.4).

FIGURE 6.4   **Example of monitoring both academic engaged time and math CBM data.**

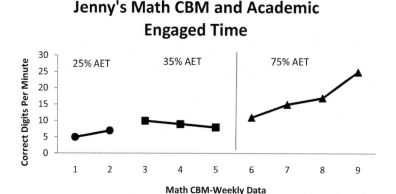

Social Skills

Another important consideration is other data available on social skills performance. As discussed in Chapter 4, daily behavior report (DBR) cards on schoolwide behavioral expectations are often collected on students who are at risk of more severe behavior problems. As seen in Figure 6.5, progress on DBRs can be graphed with CBM data. The special education teacher or other members of the data analysis team can make decisions about how behavior problems may be affecting (or related to) academic performance. Because academics and behavior are not necessarily mutually exclusive, helping a student with special needs meet behavioral expectations can improve academic performance.

Behavioral Function

The findings of an FBA or FA may be connected to a student's CBM scores. For example, presentation of difficult math content may trigger defiant behavior by the student toward the teacher or peers, resulting in the student being referred to the office or not participating in the math lesson. This is a classic escape-motivated behavior. The student finds the content difficult, would prefer not work on it, and—rather than communicate the need for assistance in a socially acceptable manner—yells at the teacher or peers and refuses all instruction, which predictably earns him or her a trip to the office. For the student, this behavior is reinforced because he or she no longer has to complete work that is difficult. In fact, no work is required at all! Figure 6.6 depicts possible functional relationships that are often discovered in the course of an FBA. Some, but not all, of the possible solutions are depicted.

Special educators and other members of IEP teams can incorporate FBA and CBM data to more comprehensively address the needs of students with academic and behavioral problems. Providing positive behavior support to address what evokes the disruptive behavior(s), teaching new skills, and modifying any reinforcing consequences can help a student engage in the curriculum and increase the likelihood that he or she can learn the desired academic skills. Specialized solutions should be identified for each student and be related to each learning context.

FIGURE 6.5   **Example of the relationship between behavioral expectations in the classroom and CBM scores for reading.**

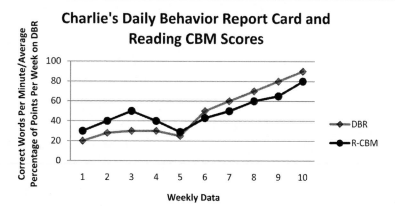

ASSISTIVE TECHNOLOGY AND RTI

Assistive technology (AT) must be considered by the IEP team according to the Individuals with Disabilities Education Improvement Act (IDEIA, 2004). A significant issue in special education when implementing RTI is how to incorporate assistive technology modifications and accommodations. We believe that the interventionist approach of RTI and the accommodation or modification approach to support are compatible. Assistive technology is used to provide compensatory support to a student. In the simplest form, a wheelchair is a compensatory support that permits a student who cannot walk to be mobile. There are many other types of AT that students may need in order to compensate for learning or behavioral disabilities. These can include, for example, computer programs that assist in writing, communication devices, and computer devices that help people follow step-by-step instructions.

The use of AT with a student is no different than any other intervention; however, in most cases, it serves only a compensatory function. The difference between an instructional intervention and a compensatory support is that the former is a learning activity for which the objective is for students to acquire knowledge based on that activity, and the latter is a device, computer technology, or other support that permits students to learn and gain access to the curriculum and their environment. Sometimes, assistive technologies not only serve as a compensatory support, but they also function as an intervention. For example, a student may need visual cues to support reading, but eventually the student learns from the pairing of the visuals and words and the support can be faded. Graphic organizers, another form of assistive technology, can help students learn to comprehend content beyond their reading level, but through systematic use may become an intervention that leads to skills development—making the assistive technology no longer necessary.

One of the most important functions of an IEP team when implementing and considering AT is testing and monitoring for effectiveness. As depicted in Figure 6.7, a concurrent probe (i.e., an assessment) is being used by the IEP team, including the special educator, to determine the usefulness of several assistive technologies. The special educator is testing different types of AT being used by a student named Stacey.

FIGURE 6.6   **Defining consequences that maintain behavior, with possible solutions.**

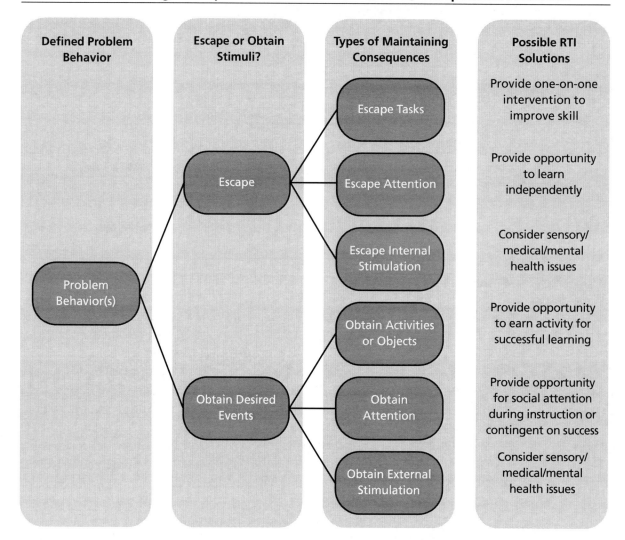

In a comprehensive model of RTI, AT assessment is an ongoing data collection process rather than an attempt to "guess" the level of effectiveness at an annual IEP meeting. As seen in Figure 6.7, there is a baseline, then an attempt at using one type of technology (the Intellitools Suite) to help the student with reading. After at least three data points are collected to establish a trend, student performance is assessed both with and without AT on the same day. The probe can be on different days if doing so will provide a more accurate assessment, but there should not be a long delay between the probes of AT and without-AT conditions. An extended delay between the two conditions could invalidate the assessment due to learning that might have occurred during that time, irrespective of the conditions.

In Stacey's graph, the data show little difference between the use of Intellitools and no AT support. The special educator concludes that Intellitools does not provide compensatory support to improve the student's performance on the CBM of reading. Stacey's performance is unresponsive to the intervention, so another should be selected. The same procedure is then repeated using a special PowerPoint-based curriculum that incorporates a direct instruction model. This supplementary program is used before the student is

FIGURE 6.7   **Example of evaluating an intervention with a concurrent probe (DI = direct instruction).**

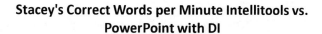

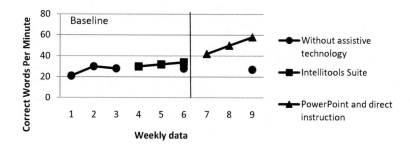

administered CBM probes and then at another point in time without the technology support. For Stacey, there is a substantial difference in performance when the PowerPoint with DI is used. This type of intervention for Stacey is ideal because it will likely serve not only as a compensatory support, but it will also be an intervention that will enhance her reading skills. At this point, the IEP team and the special education teacher can feel confident they have considered AT (consistent with the law) and they have found a technology that is effective for the student. This decision was based on data rather than guesswork.

IMPLEMENTING PROCEDURES AND INTERVENTIONS WITH INTEGRITY

All interventions or technologies have to be implemented as intended. This principle applies not only to AT procedures but to all interventions in a comprehensive RTI model. In other words, there must be *treatment integrity,* which means that the intervention is delivered to the student as intended (Peterson, Homer, & Wonderlich, 1982). Modifying a scientifically based intervention (standard protocol) may make the intervention less effective— or not work at all. It is essential, therefore, that comprehensive RTI schools design and implement methods to routinely assess treatment integrity.

Implementation of RTI requires educators to rule out the instructional causes of poor student performance. If scientifically based practices are implemented as intended, a problem-solving team or special educator can determine with some certainty whether an intervention is effective for the student. Figure 6.8 compares outcomes of a program when implemented with high treatment integrity and the same program implemented with low treatment integrity. Although a high degree of treatment integrity does not ensure successful results, it does ensure educators that students will not receive the benefits of interventions if they are not implemented as intended. It is our responsibility as educators to ensure that we choose the best interventions for students and that we implement them with 100 percent treatment integrity.

Assessing Treatment Integrity via Feedback

There are many approaches to assessment of treatment integrity in special education, inclusive, and general education classrooms. Ideally, educators work in teams. Observing

FIGURE 6.8   **Example of graphing the relationship between treatment integrity and student performance.**

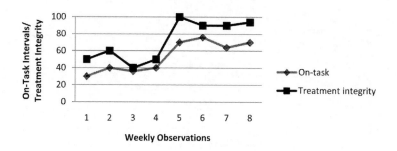

each other periodically and giving each other feedback as to the degree to which the interventionist followed the intervention protocol (i.e., the implementation steps). Making positive suggestions and sharing ideas with each other on how to adhere to protocol can improve treatment integrity (e.g., Noell, Witt, Gilbertson, Ranier, & Freeland, 1997). It can be very difficult in a busy classroom to adhere to the steps of an intervention or procedure. A student may become disruptive, class may be interrupted, a student may need special attention, or the lesson is not going as expected. These are common problems, and educators should not be discouraged if they are unable to follow the required steps of an intervention all the time, or if it takes a while to learn how to complete all of the steps.

We have found that teachers who use colleague feedback are able to help each other be more effective. We would also suggest that colleague feedback may be more effective than supervisor or principal feedback and therefore represents additional options for assessing treatment integrity. The goal of observing a teacher's implementation of an intervention is to obtain an accurate assessment of what it is like to implement the program under typical conditions. Naturally, when a supervisor is in the room, a teacher wants to appear effective. This may provide inaccurate data on how well the intervention is implemented daily because the teacher is attempting to please a supervisor. We therefore suggest that treatment integrity data not be used for the purpose of job evaluation. It is important that educators feel comfortable being observed, even if they are struggling with following the implementation requirements of a particular program. Using this type of data for a job evaluation does not build trust. Moreover, accurate data based on real circumstances will help educational teams understand the barriers to effective implementation and find creative solutions to overcome them. In special education classrooms, this can be especially true because the students may have numerous and varying needs or may exhibit challenging behavior problems. In many general and special education settings a paraprofessional is part of the educational team and shares in the intervention delivery responsibility. Just like the teacher himself or herself, the paraprofessional's treatment integrity should be monitored. The same nonthreatening conditions must exist for the observation of the paraprofessional.

Because it is impractical to have someone continually monitor treatment integrity, educators are encouraged to self-monitor treatment integrity by using a checklist. However, because it is human nature for people to want to feel like they are doing a good job, and educators want to do the best work they can for the students they serve, it is difficult to remain objective about one's own teaching. As a result, self-monitoring of treatment integrity (through the use of self-administered checklists) is typically not as accurate as peer-monitored treatment integrity. It is therefore best to use peer monitoring to increase the accuracy (i.e., the reliability) of self-monitoring. Figure 6.9 depicts a simple treatment integrity form. The form, which is provided in the appendix and on the CD that accompanies this book, can be adapted for use with any intervention. It allows for the monitoring of treatment integrity when the teacher delivers the intervention, and it also helps a teacher monitor which steps or components of the intervention are being consistently implemented. Steps that are not consistently implemented represent areas of concern, and the teacher should work with colleagues on ways to implement all of the steps consistently and as intended.

CULTURALLY AND LINGUISTICALLY DIVERSE LEARNERS

We believe that many of the same assumptions we have discussed in this chapter and throughout the book apply to the unique needs of culturally and linguistically diverse (CLD) students. However, CLD students have particular needs that differ from students who are white and/or for whom English is their first language. Because we acknowledge the importance of culturally responsive education and value cultural diversity, we firmly believe that *solid, evidence-based instruction can work for all children.* Furthermore, we believe that lack of access to effective, data-based decision making and to a rich, scientifically based educational curriculum may contribute to many of the educational difficulties historically experienced by CLD students. When CLD students have the same access to evidenced-based practices, it is likely that their performance will match that of peers from the dominant culture and those who are native speakers of the dominant language. However, cultural and linguistic social contexts in the family and community are essential to consider in the education of CDL students—just as family, community, customs, and language are critical considerations in learning for students who speak English as their first language and whose values and ethnic background are from the dominant culture in the United States.

It is important to track the effectiveness of curricular interventions for CLD learners. The Tier I universal curriculum and standard protocols for targeted interventions at Tier II should be assessed for their effectiveness with CLD students. It is possible, for example, that a Tier I universal curriculum is effective for all of the students in the building except CLD students. In that case, the Tier I curriculum needs to be adjusted such that it works for all students at the universal level. Students with CLD should not be "passed on" to Tier II, Tier III, or special education because of an ineffective curriculum at Tier I. Figure 6.10 outlines effective practices in a comprehensive RTI model providing a continuum of supports for CLD students across tiers.

Many of the practices listed in Figure 6.10 should be followed for all students. However, because CLD students are overrepresented in special education and underrepresented in gifted programs, it is essential that educators receive appropriate professional training about how to address the language challenges that English language learners face and about the influence of cultural factors on teaching and learning.

FIGURE 6.9   **Example of a treatment integrity form.**

TREATMENT INTEGRITY FORM

Implementer: _____   Intervention: _____

Observer: _____   School: _____

Student: _____   Time/Location: _____

Grade: _____   Teacher: _____

Step	Date	Date	Date	Date	Date
1.					
2.					
3.					
4.					
5.					
Daily Integrity Percentage	_____ %	_____ %	_____ %	_____ %	_____ %

Comprehensive RTI schools should have a shared responsibility for all students, including students with disabilities and CLD learners. A shared knowledge about how to provide CLD students with an education of the highest standards and that addresses any unique or remedial needs proactively and early is essential. A comprehensive RTI approach can provide the vehicle to achieve these goals. However, if the commitment to the success of all students is not infused into the culture of the school, its success in teaching students with CLD backgrounds may prove elusive. Building a positive, success-driven attitude is as important as the culturally responsive practices themselves. Finally, educators need to monitor treatment integrity to these practices and implement them with a high degree of fidelity. It is simply useless to have a positive culture in the school if the most effective practices for CLD students are not employed with integrity.

UNIVERSAL DESIGN FOR LEARNING AND COMPREHENSIVE RTI

A major theme of this chapter (and indeed this entire book) is that we need to use data to make decisions. Typically, RTI focuses on a universal or core curriculum, then a targeted curriculum matched to the needs of at-risk groups, and, if that fails, then a specially designed curriculum matched to the needs of individual students. However, an emerging model of curricula design based on some advances in neuroscience suggests that by providing multiple means of representation, expression, and engagement we can help students gain greater access to the curriculum. The guiding principles in this model are

FIGURE 6.10   **Supports by tier to address CLD learners in a comprehensive RTI model.**

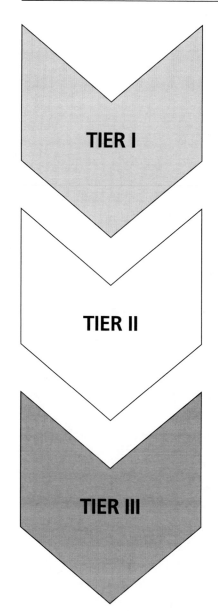

TIER I
- High expectations
- Equitable practices
- Additive views of language
- Rich and challenging curriculum
- Qualified teachers
- Focus on student strengths and building resilience
- Community outreach
- Collaboration with families
- Fidelity to practice

TIER II
- Ongoing diagnostic assessment
- Re-teach
- Monitor progress
- Build on prior knowledge
- Use small groups
- Use prescriptive teaching
- Teach skills, subject, concepts
- Provide instruction that is meaningful and comprehensible
- Design alternative programs to meet the needs of CLD students
- Fidelity to practice

TIER III
- Intensive progress monitoring
- Collaboration with families
- Community outreach
- Consider social behavior competency and support in a cultural context
- Intensive work with families, providing external agency support when needed
- Provide culturally responsive instruction in the classroom and for intensive service delivery
- Use CLD expertise on problem-solving team
- Design alternative programs to meet the needs of CLD students

referred to as universal design for learning (UDL; Center for Applied Special Technology, 2010). Universal design for learning has roots in universal design, which is a design principle of creating access to the most diverse range of individuals possible. For example, a building might have a ramp installed rather than stairs. A ramp at the proper incline is accessible to most people, even if they are wheelchair bound or have some other physical disability that makes traversing stairs difficult. Universal design for learning has the goal of creating curricula that also provide maximum access for all students.

As we have previously discussed in this chapter and elsewhere in this book, the goal of RTI is not simply to gain access to the curriculum. Rather it is to intervene to help a student or group of students achieve learning goals. Because students with disabilities and

CLD students have often been denied access to meaningful and effective educational experiences, it is natural for advocates to want these students to have increased access.

We view access as only the first step, and effective prevention and intervention are essential if students are going to make progress and if, as educators, we are ultimately able to obtain sustainable changes in learning outcomes for students. Table 6.1 shows how UDL principles can be exemplified across the tiers. It should be noted that this table is not a comprehensive list—just some examples. The goal of a quality UDL curriculum is not to overaccommodate students. For example, if a student can learn to use a computer mouse, and the objective is to learn how to do so, then it does not make educational sense to provide the student with an alternative to using a mouse. On the other hand, if a student requires educational support to use a mouse or may never possess the motor control to use a mouse, then it is defensible to provide access to different options. In UDL, these options should be readily available, and students should be encouraged to seek out different options to express themselves. Students should also be taught the pros and cons of different choices. Although using one tool may be easier at the time, in the long term the work it would take to master a specific task may have an important benefit. The older a child becomes, the more he or she can understand these choices. However, even young children can understand simple choices if presented in a developmentally appropriate manner.

SECONDARY EDUCATION

Much of the work on RTI implementation has focused on early intervention and elementary school settings. This is in part because one of the goals of RTI is to prevent problems before students reach middle school and high school. Although well intended, even the best comprehensive RTI model cannot prevent all academic or behavioral problems. In fact, some problems may not completely emerge until a student reaches secondary school. Clearly this is a neglected topic.

We start discussion of this special topic in RTI by suggesting that, although high schools and middle schools represent unique educational contexts and their students have unique developmental needs, the fundamental elements of a comprehensive RTI model remain the same. RTI in both middle school and high school includes a tiered system, uses screening and monitors progress, focuses on prevention and intervention as core educational processes that need to be in place, and addresses both academic performance and behavior.

As secondary educators contemplate how RTI can work for them, it is important that middle schools and high schools build a comprehensive RTI approach that fits their organizational and systems needs. For example, problem-solving teams may need to be organized as department or as interdisciplinary teams, depending on which would fit best for the school and the development of its students. RTI is intentionally designed to be a flexible model that can be shaped to the unique needs of secondary education.

Tiers of Instruction at the Secondary Level

One example of a secondary RTI curriculum can be drawn from the Content Literacy Curriculum (CLC) developed at the University of Kansas. Table 6.2 is an overview of CLC and contains some examples across tiers.

TABLE 6.1   Universal design for learning: Examples across tiers.

	Tier I	Tier II	Tier III
Representation Provide options for perception, language and symbols, and comprehension	Ensure that core curriculum provides options for visual input Display information in multiple formats; provide choices Permit cross-linguistic understanding Provide key concepts using nonsymbolic language	Deliver targeted intervention to provide multiple inputs Let students have access to examples that define vocabulary and symbols Ensure that targeted curriculum provides opportunities to use organizational devices; develop activities in core curriculum that enable students to use background knowledge	Provide specially designed multiple options in learning sequence that activate prior knowledge of the learner Provide specially designed multiple options that support decoding or mathematical notation Provide specially designed options that highlight critical features, big ideas, and relationships
Expression Provide options for physical action, expressive skills and fluency, and executive function	Permit different physical options to navigate core curriculum (e.g., interacting with reading program using voice, stick, or switch) Use computer-aided design to assist in problem solving Involve students in self-monitoring and goal setting related to their benchmarks	Permit students in targeted interventions to use writing software or outline tools to express answers Permit students in targeted interventions to have multiple means to support learning goal (e.g., use video) When using a computer in targeted interventions, provide alternatives to mouse control (e.g., change internal settings, use a touch screen)	Provide assistive technology devices to support writing Use specially designed procedural checklists to support students in accomplishing tasks Use specially designed think-aloud strategies to support processing
Engagement Provide options for recruiting interest, sustaining effort, and promoting self-regulation	Allow interested students the opportunity to develop parts of the core curriculum Connect curriculum goals and objectives to student goals Have all students set personal achievement goals	Focus students' attention before engaging in instruction on a targeted skill Permit students to collaborate as part of a targeted intervention Permit students to self-assess their progress during the targeted intervention	Provide choices in work sequence to decrease behavior problems Vary level of support, providing prompts when needed and independence when possible Provide specially designed coping strategy options as support for difficult school situations; vary the strategy by situational need

TABLE 6.2   Overview of the CLC multi-tiered framework for literacy (adapted from McPeak, Trygg, Minadakis, & Diana, 2007).

Tier	Effective Practice	Skill Focus	Example of Practices/Programs
Tier I	Content and strategy instruction	Develop proficiency and high-end skills that help ensure postgraduate options; consistent use of successful strategies that promote educational success	• Course mapping • Concept diagrams • Interactive study guides
Tier II	Intensive strategy instruction	Promote mastery of specific strategies across curriculum to facilitate success in identified risk areas	• Mnemonics • Test-taking strategies • Reciprocal instruction
Tier III	Basic skills instruction/therapeutic intervention	Focus on basic literacy skills with intensive support and/or underpinning of language related to content	• Corrective reading program • Failure Free Reading program

Progress Monitoring and Screening at the Secondary Level

The central focus of this book has not been on how to implement evidence-based interventions but rather how to use data to make decisions. Middle and high school students can benefit from early identification of risk factors and effective preventive responses that provide support across the tiers. A number of evidence-based interventions are available that can help students succeed (Table 6.3 contains a list of online resources to assist schools in making choices about evidence-based practices). However, to identify those needs, monitoring student progress using CBM data is essential. Tables 6.4 and 6.5 contain lists of a few screening and diagnostic tools that are useful at the secondary level for academic performance and social behavior, respectively. There are more tools than those listed, and we suggest that each district or school explore various options and research the most efficient and valid assessments for their needs.

INTERVENTIONS WITH AN EVIDENCE BASE

Effective and comprehensive assessments alone do not ensure a successful RTI model. Choosing interventions that are most likely to be effective for the students you serve is essential. What Works Clearinghouse (WWC, part of the U.S. Department of Education Institute of Education Sciences) is a highly respected resource for educational practices that have been evaluated using a rigorous scientific review process. WWC publishes its evaluations of various educational practices and standard protocols on their website at http://ies.ed.gov/ncee/wwc. However, WWC is not the only source of information about evidence-based practices. Table 6.3 lists a number of online resources to assist schools in making choices about evidence-based practices.

It is also important to note that school and district personnel need to be critical consumers of research on educational practices. Frequently, publishers of educational mate-

TABLE 6.3   Resources for selecting evidence-based practices.

Organization	Website
Council for Exceptional Children	www.cec.sped.org
National Association of School Psychologists	www.nasponline.org
National Early Childhood Technical Assistance Center	www.nectac.org/topics/evbased/evbased.asp
Center for Evidence-Based Practices	www.evidencebasedpractices.org
Florida Center for Reading Research	www.fcrr.org

rial make claims of having evidence to support practices, but the research might not have been peer reviewed or was conducted by someone with a financial interest in the outcome. As new practices and programs emerge, it is possible they may be very effective, but is also possible that the findings have been misrepresented or misinterpreted.

The following are some suggestions for evaluating evidence-based practices:

- **Consider the rigor of the** experiment. Randomized experimental design is a gold standard.

- **Determine whether the experiment was replicated.** Group design (studies with large groups of students) and single-subject design (typically three or four students) should be replicated by different researchers. Just because one researcher found that a practice worked doesn't mean we can say it will work in all situations.

- **Consider the measures employed in a study.** The measures used should be reliable and valid. Effort should have been made to establish the validity of the instrumentation used in the study. If the researchers used informal measures and did not state that they established the validity of those measures, the results should be suspect.

- **Consult experts in research design.** If the school or district does not have the expertise to evaluate studies, consider input from a consultant who does. If you use a consultant, he or she should be able to explain why an intervention is useful or not for your population of students and at each tier. He or she should be able to explain reliability, validity, and other scientific principles so that you can understand the pros and cons of any intervention or curriculum you may be considering. The consultant also should be independent. The developer of a program, for example, is not usually the best person to give advice about its quality (program developers have an inherent interest in the dissemination of the program, which produces a conflict of interest; schools want objective decision makers when selecting programs). However, once you have made the decision that it is a quality intervention, program developers/authors are excellent resources on how to implement their programs.

- **Understand that not all interventions will work for all students.** You should have multiple interventions for use with a variety of students. Therefore, you will need to select more than one program.

- **Evaluate the sources.** Because a program is on the Internet does not necessarily mean it is effective. The Internet can be a powerful tool in researching and finding interventions, but there are also many unproven educational practices disseminated online. Therefore, keep a critical eye on interventions found on the Internet.

TABLE 6.4 **Academic assessment tools for RTI in secondary schools (some content adapted from McPeak, Trygg, Minadakis, & Diana, 2007).**

Assessment	Purpose	Publisher/Secondary Grade Levels
Reading		
Analytical Reading Inventory	Screening/monitoring progress in • Listening • Comprehension • Decoding • Phonics • Fluency	Prentice Hall/6–12
Developmental Reading Assessment	Screening for • Fluency • Comprehension • Phonics	Pearson Learning Group/6–8
Lexia Comprehensive Reading Test	Screening/diagnostics/monitoring progress in • Decoding • Fluency • Phonics • Comprehension	Lexia Learning Systems/6–12
Maze Reading CBM	Screening for reading fluency	AIMSweb/6–8
Test of Reading Comprehension	Screening for comprehension and vocabulary in content areas	PRO-ED Publishing/6–12; upper age limit is 17
The Critical Reading Inventory	Screening monitoring progress in comprehension and decoding	Pearson Education–Prentice Hall/6–12
Test of Silent Word Reading Fluency (TOSWRF)	Screening/ monitoring progress in silent word fluency and decoding	PRO-ED Publishing/6–12; upper age limit is 17
Math		
Math Concepts and Application	Screening/monitoring progress; targets math-related concepts and application	System to Enhance Educational Performance (STEEP)/6–12
Math Computation Fluency	Screening/monitoring progress; targets computation skills	System to Enhance Educational Performance (STEEP)/6–12
AIMSweb Math Concepts and Applications (M-CAP)	Screening/monitoring progress in • Data and statistics • Algebra • Number sense • Operations • Patterns and relationships • Measurement • Geometry	Pearson/6–8

TABLE 6.5   Behavioral assessment tools for RTI in secondary schools.

Assessment	Purpose	Publisher/Secondary Grade Levels
Behavior		
Office Discipline Referral Tracking	Informal screening and nonspecific monitoring of progress	Various programs available, e.g., Schoolwide Information Systems (SWIS™, University of Oregon), grades K–12.
Systematic Screening for Behavior Disorders	Screening for internalizing and externalizing behavior problems	Sopris West/Some support of validity with grades 6–8
Student Risk Screening Scale	Screening for internalizing and externalizing behavior problems	T. Drummond (author)/grades 6–12
Behavior Assessment System for Children, 2nd ed.	Screening for internalizing and externalizing behavior problems	Pearson/grades 6–12
Social Skills Improvement System	Screening for internalizing and externalizing behavior problems	Pearson/grades 6–12
Daily Behavior Report Cards	Monitoring of progress; often used with computer- or Web-based data-tracking systems to monitor progress of students who need targeted or intensive interventions	Informal/grades 6–12; programs vary—School-Wide Information System (SWIS, University of Oregon) and Check, Connect, & Expect (University of Washington) are two tracking programs

SUMMARY OF IMPORTANT POINTS

□ **Special education teachers play an important role in RTI.** They serve as interventionists within an RTI model.

□ **A continuum of supports must be available in special education classrooms.** All students in special education need some level of support.

□ **RTI does not use a traditional method of assessment for special education.** For example, in a comprehensive RTI model, assessment varies in frequency and might be administered by different individuals, depending on student needs.

□ **Data-based decision making is essential in determining when a student should exit special education.** Exiting special education is possible within the RTI model, but it should be based on data that support such a decision.

□ **Functional behavior assessment (FBA) and functional analysis (FA) are important tools in special education.** They can yield critical information to special educators.

□ **Behavioral data can be relevant to academic data.** A student who struggles in a particular subject area might exhibit behavior problems related to the academic deficiency.

□ **Treatment integrity is essential in RTI.** Treatment integrity means that an intervention is delivered as intended by its developers.

◻ **Culturally and linguistically diverse (CLD) learners have unique needs.** High expectations, connections with families, and fidelity to intervention and culturally responsive educational practices are essential in providing interventions within an RTI framework to CLD learners.

◻ **Successful implementation of RTI requires the use of evidence-based practices for all students.** High-quality, evidence-based practices are beneficial for all students. Assessment and selection of appropriate evidence-based interventions are critical, and resources are available to help schools select effective interventions.

◻ **Universal design for learning principles play a role in a comprehensive RTI model.** Universal design is a method of designing and presenting a curriculum that can enhance learning access across tiers.

◻ **Secondary students can benefit from RTI.** Although RTI traditionally focuses on early education, many assessments and interventions are available for implementing a comprehensive RTI model in a middle school or high school.

REFERENCES

Brownell, M. T., Sindelar, P. T., Kiely, M. T., & Danielson, L. C. (2010). Special education teacher quality and preparation: Exposing foundations, constructing a new model, *Exceptional Children, 76*(3), 357–377.

Center for Applied Special Technology (CAST). (2010). UDL learning guidelines (Ver. 1.0). Wakefield, MA: CAST. www.cast.org/aboutudl/udlguidelines

Education for All Handicapped Children's Act, Pub. L. No. 94–142 (1975).

Fullan, M. (2007). *The new meaning of educational change* (4th ed.). New York, NY: Teacher's College Press.

Heward, W. L. (2003). Ten faulty notions about teaching and learning that hinder the effectiveness of special education. *Journal of Special Education, 36,* 186–205.

Illinois State Board of Education. (2010a). *Illinois special education eligibility and entitlement procedures and criteria within a Response to Intervention (RtI) framework: A guidance document.* www.isbe.state.il.us/spec-ed/pdfs/sped_rti_framework.pdf

Illinois State Board of Education. (2010b). *Frequently asked questions about Response to Intervention.* www.isbe.state.il.us/RtI_plan/rti_faq.pdf

Individuals with Disabilities Education Improvement Act, Pub. L. No. 108–446 (2004).

Johnston, T. C. (2010). *Data without tears: How to write measurable educational goals and collect meaningful data.* Champaign, IL: Research Press.

McPeak, L., Trygg, L., Minadakis, A., & Diana, P. (2007). *The secondary literacy instruction and intervention guide: Helping school districts transform into systems that produce life-changing results for all children.* Mill Valley, CA: The Stupski Foundation. www.stupski.org/documents/ Secondary_Literacy_Instruction_ Intervention_Guide.pdf

Miller, K. A., Gunter, P. L., Venn, M. J., Hummel, J., & Wiley, L. P. (2003). Effects of curricular and materials modifications on academic performance and task engagement of three students with emotional or behavioral disorders. *Behavioral Disorders, 28,* 130–149.

Noell, G. H., Witt, J. C., Gilbertson, D. N., Ranier, D. D., & Freeland, J. T. (1997). Increasing teacher intervention implementation in general education settings through consultation and performance feedback. *School Psychology Quarterly, 12,* 77–88.

Peterson, L., Homer, A., & Wonderlich, S. (1982). The integrity of independent variables in behavior analysis. *Journal of Applied Behavior Analysis, 15,* 477–492.

U.S. Department of Education (2006). *Twenty-eighth annual report to Congress on the implementation of the Individuals with Disabilities Education Act.* Washington, DC: U.S. Department of Education.

Wagner, M., Newman, L., Cameto, R., & Levine, P. (2006). *The academic achievement and functional performance of youth with disabilities. A report from the National Longitudinal Transition Study-2 (NLTS2).* NCESER-2006–3000. Menlo Park, CA: SRI.

ADDITIONAL SOURCES

Canter, A., Klotz, M. B., & Cowan, K. (2008). Response to Intervention: The future for secondary schools. *Principal Leadership, 8*(6), 12–15.

Crone, D. A., & Horner, R. H. (2003). *Building positive behavior supports systems in schools: Functional behavior assessment.* New York, NY: Guilford Press.

Daly, E. J., Chafouleas, S., & Skinner, C. H. (2005). *Interventions for reading problems: Designing and evaluating effective strategies.* New York, NY: Guilford Press.

Garcia, S. B., & Ortiz, A. A. (2008). A framework for the culturally and linguistically responsive design of Response to Intervention models. *Multiple Voices for Ethnically Diverse Exceptional Learners, 11*(1), 24–41.

Hughes, C., & Dehsler, D. (2007). *RTI in middle school. How will the game play out?* Washington, DC: National Center on Response to Intervention, http://www.nrcld.org/about/presentations/2007/RTI_Secondary.pdf

Lane, K., & Beebe-Frankenberger, M. (2003). *School-based interventions: The tools you need to succeed.* Boston, MA: Allyn & Bacon.

O'Neill, R. E., Horner, R. H., Albin, R. W., Sprague, J. R., Storey, K., & Newton, J. S. (1997). *Functional assessment and program development for problem behavior: A practical handbook.* Pacific Grove, CA: Brookes/Cole.

Parette, H. P., Blum, C., & Boekmann, N. (2009). Evaluating assistive technology in early childhood education: The use of a concurrent time series probe approach. *Early Childhood Education Journal, 37,* 5–12.

Rathvon, N. (1999). *Effective school interventions: Strategies for enhancing academic and social competence.* New York, NY: Guilford Press.

Simonsen, B., Shaw, S. F., Faggella-Luby, M., Sugai, G., Coyne, M. D., Rhein, B., Madaus, J. W., & Alfano, M. (2010). A schoolwide model for service delivery: Redefining special educators as interventionists. *Remedial and Special Education, 31*(1), 17–23.

CHAPTER 7

Important Considerations and Trouble Shooting in RTI

CHAPTER OVERVIEW

Based on our experiences in working with schools on implementing Response to Intervention, we know that many logistical concepts, policies, and procedures need to be worked out. Therefore, this chapter is provided as a trouble-shooting guide for developing, implementing, sustaining, and evaluating an RTI process in a school or district.

This chapter is organized according to the sequence of previous chapters—that is, we first address issues relating to the material covered in Chapter 1 (implementation and the basic process of RTI) and Chapter 2 (universal screening measures), then do the same for subsequent chapters. We believe this approach avoids overwhelming the reader with logistical information in the beginning. We also believe it is beneficial to address questions and concerns when sufficient understanding is obtained through the initial reading of each chapter.

The discussion about Chapter 1 is longest because it deals with the "meat" of logistical considerations, which are often best handled during the planning and early stages of the implementation process. The discussion for Chapters 2 through 6 is more in line with the length of the chapters themselves.

IMPORTANT CONSIDERATIONS AND LESSONS LEARNED: RTI IMPLEMENTATION (CHAPTER 1)

Instituting an RTI model occurs in six phases: (1) planning, (2) building consensus, (3) building the infrastructure, (4) implementing, (5) evaluating, and (6) sustaining and improving implementation. We address each of these phases to explain some common tasks and logistics that could facilitate or impede the process.

Phase I: Planning

Develop an Advisory Committee

Without pre-planning, the development and implementation of an RTI model will be difficult and frustrating. Our experience as consultants has shown us that schools that develop an advisory committee or planning team (which, for purposes of brevity, is called an advisory committee in this chapter) that meets regularly to discuss the implementation process are more successful. The primary functions of the advisory committee are to:

◻ Provide consistent dissemination of information.

◻ Provide uniformity in the implementation process within a district.

◻ Serve as a high-level problem-solving group for carving out a framework and institute appropriate deadlines for implementation procedures.

◻ Identify solutions to expected and unexpected challenges.

Because RTI is a general education (not special education) initiative, most of the members of the advisory committee should be general education personnel. The committee should also include individuals with decision-making power in the district, central administration staff (e.g., the assistant superintendent for curriculum and the director of special education), building-level administrators, classroom teachers from various grade levels (elementary, middle, and high school) in the district, and representatives from special and remedial education and special programs (such as reading coaches, teachers, school psychologists, and social workers), and curriculum and instruction personnel. It is also important to have at least one parent on the advisory committee.

Because it is likely that the advisory committee will experience member turnover, it is essential to have a mechanism to bring new members up to speed on the issues being addressed by the committee.

A critical function of the advisory committee is to help every member of the school community understand his or her new role in an RTI system. Resources such as position descriptions in an RTI model developed by a consortium of professional organizations should be consulted (see www.nasponline.org/advocacy/rtifactsheets.aspx).

Develop a Vision

The advisory committee should adopt a vision for RTI implementation for their district. This vision should address the purposes, goals, and expected outcomes of RTI (e.g., improved student achievement). The committee should also develop and maintain an RTI implementation action plan. The action plan should include a time line for RTI implementation and identify who is responsible for facilitating each aspect of the plan.

When developing a vision and time line, consideration should be given to discussing assets the district currently has related to RTI implementation. A needs assessment would be useful as a basis for the discussion. For example, the advisory committee could focus on what the district currently does related to assessment of all students (screening? diagnosis? accountability?) and determine how those assessments are used to drive instructional decision making. Some other questions to address in shaping a vision include the following:

◻ What is the nature of the universal curriculum?

◻ Can the district partner with any community agencies to implement interventions as part of a tiered system (church groups, senior citizen centers, parks and recreation department)? What about local businesses and industries? Large businesses often encourage their employees—and may even give them time off during the workday—to volunteer with community agencies and schools.

◻ Which central office staff are available to support the school or district in implementing RTI? What would be the roles and expectations of these staff in that regard?

◻ How are decisions made in the district, and what accountability measures are in place to monitor the building of leadership and improvement of educational outcomes?

Explore Funding Options

The advisory committee should investigate current funding sources and determine whether those sources will support RTI. If funding is based on the number of students identified for special education and if these numbers are reduced, teachers will be eliminated. That does not support implementation of RTI, which has as one of its goals the provision of more timely interventions so as to reduce chronic learning problems that in the past would have been diagnosed as mild learning disabilities. Many states have gone to "hold harmless" funding—meaning that their levels of support are based on the average number of students receiving special education services over the last five or so years. Furthermore, 15 percent of IDEA special education funds can be used to support RTI (i.e., services for students prior to being referred and found eligible for special education).

Phase II: Building Consensus

Educate Administrators

It is crucial that the administration understand and support a comprehensive approach to RTI. Without this key level of support, any RTI model will likely fail. Administrators not only need to understand the model—they also need to provide access to training, support necessary organizational changes (such as changes in schedules to allow time to implement interventions within a tiered system), and provide moral support to all school staff to help them deal with changes facing the school.

Educate and Train as Many People as Possible

Accurate information and training are paramount. RTI is a major shift in process and procedure—and so is the thinking that governs its implementation. There appears to be a relationship between the proportion of people trained within a district and positive outcomes, as well as considerably less resistance.

Control Information

The role of advisory committee members should include "reporting out" through, for example, reports on a district listserv or website and/or presentations and discussions at the building level. It is important to control rumors that often have school staff concerned that significant change is occurring without adequate planning. When "reporting out," the use of simple language should be emphasized. Avoid unclear jargon and numerous acronyms.

Present a Seamless System

It is crucial not to create RTI as separate system. RTI is meant to be dynamic and fluid, and students should not be labeled as "RTI students." Stakeholders need to understand that RTI is not an "add on" but rather represents the conceptual framework or blueprint from which all instruction (academic and behavioral) is being conducted in the district and should be integrated into other district initiatives. RTI should also be institutionalized by including the model in board of education and individual school policies; posting information on the district's website; putting information in parent, student, and staff handbooks; and discussing it in orientation meetings for these three groups of stakeholders.

Prompt People to Process

Finally, it is important to allow time for participants in training to process what they have learned. A strategy that has been reported as effective by participants of training is to allow them to compare and contrast the current model of service with the new RTI model. It is important to clearly articulate the universal curriculum (at Tier I) currently being used in the basic skills areas of reading, mathematics, written language, and behavior at all levels (elementary, middle, and high school). It is our experience that some schools do not have universal curricula or, in many cases, classroom teachers are not implementing these curricula or are implementing them with little integrity. Participants can be presented with information during training, then asked to reflect on their current practices and compare them to the presented information. Other options are to conduct teacher interviews and/or classroom observations during instructional periods in these academic skills areas, then discuss the information during training sessions.

This same form of comparing and contrasting—and perhaps discussion—should also occur when providing information about assessment and interventions, which might be conceptualized as occurring at Tier II or III. Decisions about which instructional components to continue, which to eliminate, and which to add should be based on data that reflect student outcomes. Schools and educators should not be asked to refrain from using instructional practices that are effective in terms of student outcomes.

Phase III: Building the Infrastructure

Build the RTI System Slowly

The mantra that we often chant is you must move slow to move fast. It is important to do it right (or as close to right as possible) the first time. School personnel must keep in mind that RTI is a process and should be built over time with integrity. Schools need to build the overall RTI system slowly. School personnel often become excited about the possibilities of RTI and begin implementing universal screening measures for reading, mathematics, written expression, and behavior all at once. In doing so, much is often missed with regard to integrity of the implementation of the process, or the process becomes too overwhelming and is abandoned or is conducted with less integrity.

Assess Technological Needs

Technology is critical to successful implementation of an RTI model. A work group should be established by the advisory committee to discuss technology needs—particularly those related to data-based decision making. Technology can make data collection more efficient and reduce paperwork. Principals and teachers should be included in this work group to ensure that the technology adopted is user friendly.

Phase IV: Implementing RTI

Keep in Mind That Training Is Critical

With the implementation of RTI, there should be "no staff left behind" in terms of providing an opportunity to learn the skills necessary to implement this initiative. Coaching models of professional development are more effective than "one-shot," in-service presentations. Point people for technical assistance and problem solving should be identified. Skill sets (taught to internal coaches who then provide professional development to school staff) that are critical for full implementation of RTI include the following:

- ◻ The ability to use an ecological approach in understanding student academic and behavioral problems. This includes recognizing the importance of modifying the instructional environment to develop students' academic and behavior skills.
- ◻ An understanding of curriculum-based measurement and principles of effective monitoring of student progress.
- ◻ The ability to collect observational data.
- ◻ The ability to monitor the effectiveness of interventions.
- ◻ Knowledge of effective behavioral and instructional principles.
- ◻ Knowledge of a variety of evidence-based standard protocol treatments for developing academic and behavior skills.
- ◻ The ability to conduct functional behavior assessments.
- ◻ An understanding of systematic problem solving, including skills in problem identification, problem analysis, plan development, plan implementation, and plan evaluation.
- ◻ The ability to analyze why a problem is occurring and to implement research-based instructional practices.
- ◻ An understanding of the principles of single-case research design.
- ◻ The ability to implement effective teaming and collaborative consultation.

Work with Others When Possible

The implementation process is likely to be more challenging when done alone. It is often helpful for multiple schools, either in districts or cooperatives, to work together in solving logistical concerns.

Keep RTI as the Primary Focus

The implementation of RTI can facilitate a school district in fulfilling its mission and vision, and in reaching its academic and social-emotional/behavioral goals related to educating its students. The RTI plan that is developed should be incorporated into the school improvement plan (SIP) for the particular school that is implementing RTI.

Phase V: Evaluating RTI

Develop an Evaluation Plan

The advisory committee should discuss and develop an evaluation plan and data collection system based on their vision, objectives, and expected outcomes for the RTI model being implemented in their district. The evaluation plan should focus on student outcomes but also include school personnel, parent, and student satisfaction measures. Before evaluating student outcomes, a plan to assess and ensure treatment integrity at all three tiers should be developed. Often, educational initiatives are not found to lead to positive student outcomes—not because they are not good ideas but because they were not implemented as intended in the first place.

Develop Evaluation Materials

An evaluation may include multiple components, depending on the goals set in developing an RTI model. For example, a school may have as an intended outcome of RTI that parents become more involved with the process. It is important that the school be able to measure its performance toward that goal. Two other common areas to be evaluated are RTI teams (self-evaluation) and actual fidelity of RTI processes (conducted by an external evaluator). The point here is that if there is a specific goal established, the RTI advisory team should have a method of measuring progress toward that goal. Toward that end, the Recommended Resources section at the end of this chapter contains links to online resources for questionnaires and other evaluation tools.

Phase VI: Sustaining and Improving RTI

Use Your Evaluation Data

Based on the results of the evaluation(s) of RTI implementation, modifications can, if necessary, be made in the system. The goal then becomes sustaining the initiative. RTI inherently includes a feedback system; therefore, results from the various assessments and monitoring of interventions developed and implemented at each of the three tiers enable decisions to be made as to what aspects of the RTI model need to be modified as part of sustaining the implementation.

IMPORTANT CONSIDERATIONS AND LESSONS LEARNED: UNIVERSAL SCREENING MEASURES (CHAPTER 2)

Use a True Universal Screening Measure

Many people we have worked with on implementing RTI believe that they are already "doing RTI." That is, they have a method of assessment for all students. Although it generally does not take long to determine that they indeed do have a method of assessment, that method usually is what we refer to as a diagnostic tool. Diagnostic tools are more expensive and require more time to administer (generally 45 minutes or longer), which is a lot of time to spend with each student. We therefore point them back to the idea of screening and the need to reduce the number of students who require an in-depth assessment.

Select Appropriate Times for Data-Based Decision Making

There are at least eight major times at which data-based decision making needs to take place: at screening, identification, and evaluation at each of the three tiers (six decisions) and at the individual and group level (two decisions). It is helpful to schedule these activities on the school calendar, designate who is responsible for the components, and choose a method for disseminating the findings to all stakeholders in the RTI process.

Make Decisions Related to State and National Laws/Regulations

Data-based decision making can be more easily understood when it is explained in relation to No Child Left Behind (NCLB) and adequate yearly progress (AYP). NCLB requires each school to conduct annual academic assessments and report to the public on its effectiveness in meeting AYP (based on the percentage of students who meet predetermined benchmarks on statewide assessments).

Develop Local Cut Scores/Benchmarks

By developing cut scores on school-specific universal screening measures for academic performance, schools can more easily and reliably identify students at risk for academic failure.

Use a Multi-Step Process for Identifying Social Behavior Concerns

A multi-step system is ideal for identifying students at risk for social behavior problems. This process includes collecting data on office discipline referrals, using teacher rankings or nominations, and implementing additional screening measures.

Manage Data Effectively and Efficiently

By using a computer- or Web-based program to track and analyze data, schools can become more effective and efficient in identifying universal curriculum and instruction needs, as well as in identifying students at risk for both academic and behavioral problems.

Encourage Teachers to Collect Their Own Data

Some proponents of RTI encourage use of a schoolwide assessment teams (SWAT) for universal data collection. The rationale is that SWATs relieve teachers of the burden of data collection. However, there is much to be gained by having teachers collect the data. First, teachers can get firsthand experience in collecting useful data at the school, small-group, and individual levels. Second, teachers can more efficiently score and enter their data into a spreadsheet or other data management system than a SWAT can. The SWAT might have only a few people entering and scoring data for all students, which could translate into thousands of pieces of data to enter per SWAT member. In our experience, teachers strongly value the efficiency of data being returned to them for their use. Third, these data will become more meaningful to teachers as they begin to make educational decisions during grade-level team meetings (discussed in Chapter 5). Finally, simply providing teachers the opportunity to become increasingly involved with data-based decision making may facilitate ownership and "buy-in" to the RTI process.

IMPORTANT CONSIDERATIONS AND LESSONS LEARNED: DIAGNOSTIC TOOLS (CHAPTER 3)

Train Everyone Early and Often

We have found that the better people understand the importance of having two "tests"—that is, a universal screening measure (USM) and a diagnostic tool (DT)—the more readily they will work together in solving problems using the data from these "tests." Early in the RTI implementation process, many school personnel are confused about the use of USMs and DTs. By reiterating to school personnel that DTs are used to confirm USM findings for intervention selection purposes, they often not only begin to understand the process—but they also are more willing to facilitate it.

Provide Quality Professional Development

School personnel often lack the training required for individual diagnostic assessment. Although some personnel, such as school psychologists and social workers, might understand such procedures, many come from more traditional models of training that emphasize assessment and generic recommendations. We find that administrators who make a commitment to high-quality professional development of teachers and support personnel generally see more efficient and effective implementation of RTI. Much of this quality professional development takes place during school improvement plan (SIP) days. In fact, in the most highly effective schools, all SIP days are spent covering topics related in some way to the broader perspective of RTI.

In addition to SIP days, successful implementation of RTI also seems to be related to attendance at professional development opportunities away from the school. Allowing teachers and support personnel to attend professional conferences may seem expensive in the beginning, but the amount of learning that can occur and subsequently be shared with everyone else in the building (perhaps during an SIP day that usually requires a paid outside speaker) may be certainly worth the expense.

Combine Functional Behavior Assessment with Functional Analysis

Problem-solving teams are often faced with the challenge of completing functional behavior assessments (FBAs) or functional analyses (FAs) for Tier III and special education levels of service delivery. As consultants, we increasingly find that we are likely to do a bit of both rather than simply one or the other. There are two reasons we often do both. First, we can expedite the functional analysis by *not* testing each of the four functions of behavior. Often, we find that the hypotheses of tangible reinforcement and sensory reinforcement as causes of problem behaviors can be eliminated after utilizing functional assessment methods such as teacher interviews and behavior description recording. Second, we cannot always clearly determine the function of behavior but can narrow it down to two through a functional assessment. We therefore test only two of the hypotheses typically conducted in a functional analysis. By combining components of FBA with FA we (1) reduce the amount of time required to complete an FA alone, (2) confirm hypotheses with FA that we would have not otherwise confirmed with FBA alone, and (3) end up with multiple data sources converging to guide our decisions (from observations, interviews, experimental manipulations, etc.).

Make Data Collection Easy for Teachers

Being a teacher requires juggling many activities, and even expert teachers may find it a challenge to collect data. As consultants, we have found that providing teachers with simple methods for collecting data results in higher data collection efficacy and integrity. Here are six tips for problem-solving teams to keep in mind when asking teachers to collect data:

◻ Never ask a teacher to collect data that he or she is not sufficiently trained to collect.

◻ Never ask a teacher to collect data that you wouldn't be able or willing to collect yourself. The true test is this: If the teacher says no, then a member of the problem-solving team should collect it.

◻ Have teachers collect only the data they think are helpful or reliable. If teachers are going to use a simple frequency count, encourage them to collect these data when they think they will see the behavior and when data collection will not be burdensome.

◻ Have teachers use easy and inconspicuous methods of data tallying. Making tally marks on a board, on their arms with pen, or an index card at their desk has obvious limitations. Having teachers "count" observations of behavior by moving paper clips from the left pocket to the right pocket, or turning pages in a book for every instance and noting how many page turns were made for a specified period of time allows the teacher to easily keep track of behavior occurring in the classroom and minimizes reaction from students.

◻ Do not have teachers collect data using systematic behavior observation recording methods. This requires too much effort, time, and experience to be reliable and meaningful.

◻ Do not have teachers use descriptive behavior recording procedures for high-frequency behavior (that is, a behavior that occurs more than once every 5 minutes). For a high-frequency behavior, it is best to ask the teacher to collect frequency count data and have an observer collect data using behavior description recording or systematic, direct behavior observation recording procedures.

IMPORTANT CONSIDERATIONS AND LESSONS LEARNED: MONITORING PROGRESS (CHAPTER 4)

Give Proper Consideration to Resource Allocation

Although setting goals for the number of students to be provided services relative to some pre-determined model (e.g., 80 percent for Tier I, 10 percent for Tier II, 5 percent for Tier III, and 5 percent for special education) may seem like a valiant effort to provide appropriate services to all students, it may not be feasible. For example, a low-functioning school may find that only 20 percent of students are meeting the expectations of the Tier I curriculum. This suggests that 80 percent of students should be receiving supplemental instruction in the form of Tier II or Tier III interventions, or special education.

If following the standard rule—to provide additional services to struggling or at-risk students—would be overly taxing to the school budget, we recommend doing two things. First, consider changing the universal instruction to better identify the gaps in instruction that may account for the poor performance of so many students. One way to identify instructional variables that may need to be more intensely emphasized is to do an instructional analysis. Second, it is important to then answer the question, "How many students can we afford to intervene on behalf of, given the resources we currently have?" If the answer is 20 percent, then Tier II intervention should begin for the lowest 20 percent of the population (based on dual discrepancy).

Provide Training in Using Data

A good understanding of data is required in order to successfully evaluate RTI components. It is our perspective, unfortunately, that most training programs for school personnel do not adequately provide such an understanding. Whether collecting and analyzing data, making decisions based on universal screening measures, or having problem-solving teams complete self-assessments of their own effectiveness, there is no doubt that everyone needs to be involved and fully understand his or her role in the RTI progress monitoring and evaluation plan. Training on how to collect, input, analyze, and make decisions with data will help school personnel be more competent and effective in dealing with concerns about student academic performance and behavior. If school personnel do not understand this process and do not obtain training, the decisions they make may be faulty and result in negative outcomes. We suggest that, in the beginning stages of RTI, as many in-service days as possible be spent explaining the importance and correct use of data in making decisions.

Manage Data Effectively and Efficiently

It is critical to use computer software to manage data. Data management software allows you to:

◻ Keep all data together.

◻ Conduct sophisticated analyses.

◻ Access data quickly.

◻ Sort and/or filter data with ease.

Although many programs are used for data management, it is important for a school to choose software programs that are right for its needs. In our experience, the most sophisticated data analyzers use multiple software tools. For example, SPSS® may be used for statistical analysis, Microsoft Excel® for graph construction, AIMSweb for academic data, and SWIS™ for social behavior data. Although each program offers a variety of tools and functions, most people have preferences about how data are stored, retrieved, displayed, and printed.

Establish Schoolwide Expectations

It is helpful to monitor school functioning with regard to social behavior by establishing three to five schoolwide expectations, as suggested in a Positive Behavioral Interventions and Supports (PBIS) approach. These expectations may be things such as "Be safe," "Be respectful," and "Be ready." By setting expectations, educators can document which expectation was violated and resulted in an office discipline referral. This information, in turn, allows for data analysis to be conducted as a function of the expectations. If, for example, the "Be ready" expectation is being violated more regularly than the others, stronger emphasis can be placed on directly teaching social behavior consistent with that expectation at the building, grade, class, or individual student level. This is one example of using a systematic method to link data to intervention solutions.

IMPORTANT CONSIDERATIONS AND LESSONS LEARNED: PROBLEM-SOLVING TEAMS (CHAPTER 5)

Remember: No Data, No Meeting

It should be abundantly clear by now that we seriously ascribe to the notion that data are critical to successful implementation of RTI. It is simply not possible to make an effective decision without data. We therefore have a golden rule when it comes to problem-solving meetings: If there are no data, then there is no meeting. It might be a good idea to require various team members to bring different types of data to meetings and share them with the team as part of their roles and responsibilities. We assure you: The first time the building administrator says at the beginning of a meeting, "We have no data here, so we cannot make decisions; therefore, we should not have a meeting," things will change and people will come to meetings prepared with data.

Ensure That Problem Solving Occurs at All Tiers

To be consistent with a fully implemented RTI model, problem solving must occur at all three tiers. If not, teams become overwhelmed with the numbers of students and the intensity of needs to be addressed at any one level. For example, at the Tier III level, many teams focus on individual students and limit their actions to deciding only whether to conduct a full evaluation to determine a student's eligibility and entitlement for special education. When teams become overloaded with students who require individualized and intensive evaluations, there is little time left to address needs at Tiers I and II, which, if effective, would reduce the numbers of students at Tier III.

Use the Behavioral Consultation Model and Focus on Techniques of Behavioral Analysis

Most effective problem-solving teams within an RTI framework use methods associated with the behavioral consultation model and focus on techniques of behavior analysis. When teams do not adopt a behavioral orientation to problem solving (i.e., they do not define problems in behavioral terms), they tend to focus on variables that are more internal to the student and therefore less amenable to change.

Implement Multiple Teams

Except in very small schools, it is most effective to use multiple teams. All of the teams need a common focus of finding solutions to student, classroom-, or building-level problems. The teams should be familiar with the types of curricula and instruction delivered, the specific interventions used with small groups or individual students, and the level of supports necessary for students to be successful. When one team has to do all of the work, its members frequently become overwhelmed and discouraged. Having multiple teams distributes the workload more equitably.

Include All Stakeholders on Tier I Teams

Membership of the Tier I team should consist of all stakeholders at the building level (such as the building administrator), a parent representative (individual student data are not discussed at this level, so confidentiality is not an issue), general education teachers from different grade levels, a special education teacher, a content expert in the areas of reading and math (or other areas), and school service personnel who are familiar with data collection and analysis. Avoid having the majority of Tier I team members from special education; otherwise, RTI will be viewed as a special education—rather than general education—initiative. In addition, there will be less "buy-in" for change at the universal curriculum level if not all stakeholders are included on a Tier I team.

Organize Tier II Teams Around Grade Levels

Tier II teams are most effective when organized around grade levels and focused primarily on:

- □ Reviewing data from universal screening.
- □ Choosing targeted Tier I interventions to be delivered through differentiated instruction.
- □ Selecting particular interventions and working out logistical aspects of their delivery.
- □ Choosing students to participate in Tier II standard protocol interventions and monitoring their progress through data-based decision making.

Grade-level teams should also coordinate with the Tier I team when suggesting changes to the core curriculum based on grade-level needs. All teachers at a particular grade level (or combination of grade levels if the school is small and has, for example, only one teacher at each grade level) should participate on Tier II teams in order to achieve "buy-in" for implementing classwide universal curricular changes and small-group interventions that are often carried out by classroom teachers. It is also helpful to include a person familiar with data collection and analysis, such as the school psychologist, a content specialist in reading and/or math, and perhaps the principal.

Limit the Number of Members on Tier III Teams

Tier III team members should range in number from four to eight and should include the classroom teacher of the student being discussed, a special education teacher, the school psychologist, and a social worker—all of whom are knowledgeable about problem solving and developing more intensive interventions to address a variety of academic and social-emotional/behavioral problems. Having more than eight members leads to less efficient and effective problem solving because the group becomes too unwieldy. Groups larger than eight typically have fewer members actively participating in problem solving, and the length of meetings increases significantly. The student's parents or guardians are also valuable members of the Tier III team because they know their child best and can provide useful insights as to the causes of various school-based concerns. Parents can also implement at home the interventions developed by the Tier III team.

Note: Teams at all three tiers should have the option of inviting individuals with particular areas of expertise, depending on the nature of the issues being discussed.

Cycle Through All Five Stages of Problem Solving

When engaging in comprehensive problem solving, it is important that the team complete each of the five stages: problem identification, problem analysis, plan development, plan implementation, and plan evaluation. When stages are skipped, problem solving is less effective.

Specify the "Significant Gap" Before Evaluating the Plan

Although there are several methods for determining whether a significant gap is occurring (for example, if a student's level of performance is two times or more below the benchmark), it is important that the team specify how this gap will be determined. The reliability or consistency of decisions across student populations and the effectiveness of the decisions made are significantly improved if these decisions are made in advance of a meeting.

State the Purpose and Stages of Problem Solving

To facilitate successful outcomes at the problem identification stage, the purpose for a meeting should be made clear at the start of the meeting. Next, the stages of problem solving should be introduced and clarified, both orally and in written form, such as on a large poster. The relevant stage should be noted as the team engages in each phase of problem solving. When this advice is followed, team members tend to be more actively engaged in problem solving, and meetings are efficient because discussion stays focused.

Collect Schoolwide Benchmark and Baseline Data Before the Problem Identification Stage

Schoolwide benchmark and baseline data (for an individual or group of students) should be collected before convening a team meeting for the purpose of problem identification. Effective decision making at all stages of problem solving requires a clear understanding about where the students of interest perform in comparison to their peers.

Correctly Identify the Problem

Problem identification is the most critical stage of problem solving. Critical aspects of problem identification include operationally defining the problem behavior in behavioral terms, identifying the replacement behavior, and collecting baseline data. If the problem is not adequately identified, successful resolution cannot occur because all other stages of problem solving depend on a clear definition of the problem and a target behavior(s) the team wants to see improved.

Do Not Omit Problem Analysis in a Rush to Develop Interventions

The second stage of problem solving—problem analysis—is often omitted when problem-solving teams rush to develop and implement interventions. Without comprehensive discussion during problem analysis and development of a plan related to a confirmed hypothesis, an intervention at any tier, no matter how well designed, will be unsuccessful.

Focus on Things You Can Change

To improve outcomes during the problem analysis stage, the team should focus on correctly identifying factors that contribute to the problem. The team should eliminate factors that are not supported by the data collected. Also, they should avoid focusing solely on individual student factors that teams typically have little control over and trying to find a cause within the student. Instead, they should focus on the factors that can be changed.

Specify Decision-Making Rules Before the Plan Evaluation Meeting

Decision-making rules for the final stage of problem solving—plan evaluation—should be explicitly specified as part of the plan development stage. If these rules have not been specified, final decisions related to continuing, intensifying, or discontinuing an intervention are less reliable and effective.

Determine Specifics for Monitoring Progress During the Plan Development Stage

During the plan development stage, the team must decide which materials and standard protocols will be used for monitoring progress, when and how often data will be collected, where data will be collected, and who will collect the data. If progress monitoring data are not collected with a high degree of reliability and validity, the team cannot determine whether a particular intervention or plan has been effective, nor can they determine whether it should be continued, intensified, or discontinued.

Avoid Having Only Special Education Staff Implement Interventions

Do not rely solely on special education staff for development and implementation of all interventions; otherwise, the problems will be viewed as those to be solved by special education staff, which will consequently overextend those personnel.

Support Intervention Implementers and Assess Integrity of the Plan During Plan Implementation

During the plan implementation stage, it is important to support the intervention implementers, frequently observe interventions being implemented, and use an intervention integrity checklist to ensure that the plan has been implemented as intended. If an intervention is not implemented with a high degree of fidelity, the team cannot accurately assess its effectiveness, and all decisions based on the progress monitoring data collected will be flawed. To ensure intervention integrity at the Tier III level, a case manager should be assigned and meet with the intervention implementer within two days of the start of a new intervention.

Convene a Tier III Team Meeting Shortly After a Referral Is Made

Tier III teams should meet within 1 or 2 weeks after a request for assistance has been received from a teacher. This allows time for the team to collect problem identification and analysis data. If a more extended time lag occurs between the referral and the team meeting, teachers will become discouraged and might refrain in the future from referring students to the team. Teachers might also refer students (or encourage a student's parents or guardians to make the referral) for a special education evaluation, which will place pressure on the school to conduct an evaluation when it may not be necessary. This, in turn, will reduce "buy-in" for the RTI framework in your building and significantly compromise the integrity and effectiveness of RTI.

Adopt Formal Written Procedures and Make Them Available to Stakeholders

A manual, including a mission statement; an explanation of the school's problem-solving process; logistics (including regular meeting times and places); membership; roles and responsibilities of team members at the different tiers; and forms should be developed and distributed to all staff members. A brochure outlining the purposes of and steps in problem solving should be provided to all parents. Without such formalization and institutionalization, the problem-solving process will be less consistently implemented and less effective.

IMPORTANT CONSIDERATIONS AND LESSONS LEARNED: SPECIAL TOPICS (CHAPTER 6)

Remember That Everyone Is a Team Member

One of the unique requirements (which is also a major advantage) of RTI is that everyone in the school needs to be part of the process in order for it to be successful. With RTI, no longer is there a special education team and a general education team. There is just one team: the student outcome team. The RTI model provides opportunities for everyone to contribute to the success of all students. General educators can help with special education students, and special educators can help with general education students. Because RTI is on a continuum, the classic line between general and special education is not necessary.

Help Staff Adapt to Role Changes

Some educators might have difficulty understanding and accepting the change in their roles and with the overall change to an interventionist model. It is important to acknowledge that role and systems changes can be difficult for people. Educators may experience a sense of loss about the way things were in the past. Keeping the most effective practices and acknowledging educators' feelings can minimize this problem. Teachers should also support each other. They can help each other understand the changes, be sensitive to feelings of resistance, and help everyone focus on the big picture rather than on the challenge of making small changes in behavior. The bottom line is that a well-executed, comprehensive RTI model will help support *all* students and teachers more effectively.

Build a Comprehensive Data System

Training in data collection must be consistent across general and special education. All teachers should be trained in the various methods of data collection. It is also important that general educators and special educators know how to speak to each other about data. It is a good practice to form teams that break down traditional barriers and permit general and special educators to learn to communicate with each other about data. Ultimately, interactions between special and general educators about data should become part of their regular routines.

Develop Staff Capability in Functional Behavior Analysis

As with understanding data, skills in functional behavior analysis (FBA) should be developed in both general and special educators. Knowledge of basic functions can help everyone better understand student behavior. This type of "cross training" gives general and special educators a common language and an improved understanding of all students' behavior.

Maintain Commitment to Fidelity

Highly developed data systems and the capacity for all educators to use them are essential in a comprehensive RTI model. So is a commitment to fidelity. It is important for educators to understand that their role is to provide high-quality, evidence-based practices and to do so with fidelity. Therefore, it is vital to foster, as part of the school culture, a commitment to openness about needs and to helping each other become more efficient and fluent in using interventions.

Maintain Commitment to Equity

It is important to maintain a commitment to overcoming the inequities that produce significant educational gaps between white, middle-class students and various culturally and linguistically diverse (VCLD) students. Through data collection and effective practice, RTI can provide significant ammunition to address this problem that plagues our society. However, without the fundamental belief that all students can achieve, the promotion of high standards, and student access to meaningful and effective curriculum, it will be difficult to obtain positive outcomes for CLD students.

Integrate Universal Design for Learning

Universal design for learning (UDL) is an important and promising practice to enhance access and outcomes for children with disabilities. However, it is a relatively new concept in education. Unless a school has used UDL in the past, doing so probably should not be one of the first steps taken when implementing RTI. It would also be advisable to work with a university partner or consultant when adopting UDL. Finally, collecting data on this innovation is essential to its successful implementation.

Understand How to Implement RTI at the Secondary Level

When implementing RTI at the secondary level, it is necessary for it to fit the mission and structure of the school. Although this may seem like belaboring the obvious, it is a point sometimes missed. RTI in secondary schools looks different from that in elementary schools. There are common elements at both levels (e.g., monitoring progress, screening, tiers of interventions), but the goals and structure of secondary education are different from those of elementary education. Hence, RTI should look different at the secondary level and should be suited to the setting.

Sometimes, secondary educators might feel that RTI is attempting to impose an "elementary" teaching method on secondary students. Nothing could be further from the truth. RTI is only a framework. At the middle-school level, teams might work interdepartmentally by grade level; in a high school, teams might be structured departmentally by grade level. However, other team structures might be considered, depending on the school. Secondary educators have the flexibility to design an RTI model to suit the needs of their students.

RECOMMENDED RESOURCES

Evaluation Tools for Response to Intervention

Florida Problem Solving & Response to Intervention

www.floridarti.usf.edu/resources/program_evaluation/index.html

Parent Satisfaction Survey and Other Evaluation Tools

Illinois Alliance for School-Based Problem Solving and Intervention Resources in Education (I-ASPIRE)

www.luc.edu/cseit/i-aspireresourcesforcoordinator.shtml

APPENDIX

Reproducibles and Templates

GRAPHING WITH MICROSOFT EXCEL®

By Gary L. Cates, Ph.D.

Note: The following instructions were written for users of Microsoft Excel® 2007 and 2010. Those who use previous versions of Excel should be able to easily adapt these instructions.

Setting Up the Data

1. Open Microsoft Excel.

2. In cell A1, type `Session`

3. In cell B1, type `Baseline` (this will be where you type in baseline data only).

4. In cell C1, type `Treatment 1` (this will be where you type in Treatment 1 data only).

5. In cell D1, type `Treatment 2` (this will be where you type in Treatment 2 data only).

6. In cell A2, type the number `1`

7. In cell A3, type the number `2`

8. Highlight cells A2 and A3 by clicking on cell A2 with the left mouse button and then holding it down as you drag over to cell A3, then release the mouse button.

9. Grab onto the bottom right corner of cell A3 by left-clicking on it and holding down on the left mouse button. Now, while still holding the mouse button, drag your cursor to cell A21, then let go. This should have filled in all of your cells under the Session column with a sequential list of numbers (1–20) to represent session number.

10. In cell B2, type `#N/A` and hit Enter.

11. Now, right-click on cell B2 and choose "Copy" from the contextual pop-up menu.

12. Highlight all of the remaining cells (B2–B21 through D2–D21), then right-click and choose "Paste" from the contextual pop-up menu. You should now have "#N/A" in all of the cells under the Baseline, Treatment 1, and Treatment 2 columns.

You now have a worksheet in which you can graph baseline and treatment data for two treatments. Now let's have some real fun and input data.

Constructing the Graph

1. Click on the Insert tab and choose "Scatter with Straight Lines" from the Charts menu.

2. Right-click on the newly created (blank) chart and choose "Move Chart."

3. Select "As New Sheet" and give it a name (e.g., Graph).

4. Now click on this new sheet, then right-click on the blank graph and choose "Select Data."

From *Effective RTI Training and Practice: Helping School and District Teams Improve Academic Performance and Social Behavior,* © 2011 Gary L. Cates, Craig Blum, and Mark E. Swerdlik. Champaign, IL: Research Press (800-519-2707, www.researchpress.com)

5. Click on the tab in the spreadsheet that has your data in it. This will open up the data and allow you to select the data you want graphed. Be sure that your cursor in the "Chart data range" field is after the "=" sign.

6. In this case, the data you want to graph are the baseline data for the individual student you isolated. Simply left-click, then hold and drag down through data points (A1:A20).

7. You also will want to graph the intervention data. Simply click "Add" on the pop-up menu. In the next pop-up dialog box, put your cursor in the Y values field and clear out anything that is in there. Now go back to your data tab and select all intervention (B1:B20) data. Click OK.

8. **Optional Step (provides for more graph space):** Right-click on the series legend at the right of the graph and choose "Delete."

9. Now click once in the middle of the graph. In the main menu fields (top of the Microsoft Excel window), select the Layout tab in the Chart Tools section. Select the Gridlines icon, go to "Primary Horizontal Gridlines" and choose "None."

10. Under the same tab (Chart Tools/Layout), select the Axis Titles icon, and choose "Primary Horizontal Axis Title," then "Title Below Axis." You will notice that the X axis on your chart now reads "Axis Title." If you click on those words in your chart, you can change it to read whatever you specify (e.g., Intervention Sessions).

11. If you wish to change the font of your axis title, right-click on the axis title text to bring up a contextual menu. You can choose "Font" to change the font, the font size, font color, and other font characteristics. Click OK when you're done.

12. Repeat steps 10 and 11 for the primary vertical axis. This time choose "Rotated Title." (The name of this axis title is whatever dependent variable you are measuring (e.g., Words Read Correctly per Minute).

13. Right-click on the Y axis and choose "Format Axis" from the contextual menu that appears. Click Fixed for the major unit and change it to 5. For the maximum unit, change to Fixed and 100 as well.

14. Right-click on the X axis and choose "Format Axis" on the contextual menu that appears. Click Fixed for the major unit and change it to 1.

15. Next, select the Insert tab at the top of the Excel window. Select the Shapes icon. You can choose from among many shapes. The shape you are looking for is a line with an arrow. By selecting that shape, you can draw an arrow to point at series 1 and another arrow to point at series 2.

16. Under the Layout tab (under Chart Tools), choose the Text Box icon. Click on your graph and type, inside this new text box, the word "Baseline." If you need to move the text box (which, in this case, is serving as a phase label) so that it appears next to a respective phase, you can simply grab it and move it and/or resize it. Repeat this labeling process for each data series (Baseline, Treatment 1, Treatment 2).

Congratulations!

The following page contains an example of a spreadsheet and chart. The CD that accompanies this book contains an Excel file with sample data and a chart, which you can adapt for your own use.

Model of What Data Might Look Like in Your Spreadsheet

Session	Baseline	Treatment 1	Treatment 2
1	56	#N/A	#N/A
2	58	#N/A	#N/A
3	57	#N/A	#N/A
4	#N/A	69	
5	#N/A	#N/A	72
6	#N/A	80	
7	#N/A	#N/A	84
8	#N/A	81	
9	#N/A	#N/A	88
10	#N/A	78	
11	#N/A	#N/A	92
12	#N/A	84	
13	#N/A	#N/A	96
14	#N/A	#N/A	#N/A
15	#N/A	#N/A	#N/A
16	#N/A	#N/A	#N/A
17	#N/A	#N/A	#N/A
18	#N/A	#N/A	#N/A
19	#N/A	#N/A	#N/A
20	#N/A	#N/A	#N/A

Chart Generated from Example Data

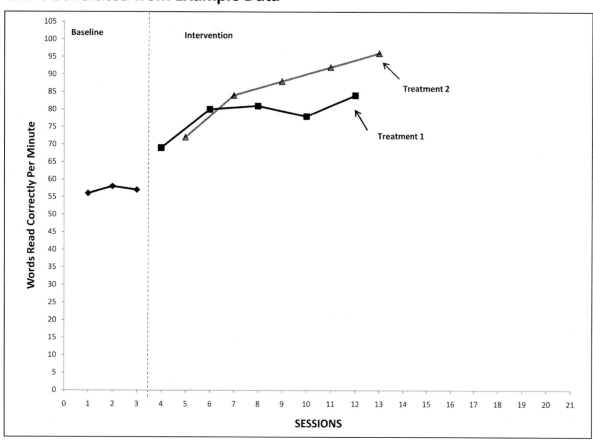

OFFICE DISCIPLINE REFERRAL FORM

Student: _____ Grade: _____ Referring Staff: _____

Date of Referral: _____ Time of Behavior: _____

LOCATION	EXTERNALIZING BEHAVIOR	INTERNALIZING BEHAVIOR
☐ Classroom #____ ☐ Hallway ☐ Cafeteria ☐ Library ☐ Bathroom _____ ☐ Bus ☐ Open yard ☐ In front of school ☐ Parking lot ☐ Other (please specify): _____ _____	☐ Abusive language ☐ Physical contact ☐ Sexual language toward peer or adult ☐ Lying ☐ Cheating ☐ Vandalism ☐ Smoking ☐ Truant from class ☐ Other (please specify): _____ _____	*For internalizing referrals, send form to office with a description of the problem, but do not send student to the office unless necessary.* ☐ Does not talk with peers ☐ Excessively shy/withdrawn ☐ Avoids social interaction ☐ Appears fearful in nonthreatening situations ☐ Fails to assert self ☐ Unresponsive to social situations ☐ Does not participate in social activities ☐ Other (please specify): _____ _____
ANTECEDENT	**BEHAVIOR**	**CONSEQUENCE**

Comments:

_____
_____
_____
_____
_____
_____
_____
_____
_____

INSTRUCTIONAL ANALYSIS FORM

Teacher: _____ Grade: _____

Subject: _____ Date: _____

Skill	Teaching Strategy	Materials	Format	Allocated Time	Reward or Reinforcer	Method of Assessment

Comments:

From *Effective RTI Training and Practice: Helping School and District Teams Improve Academic Performance and Social Behavior*, © 2011 Gary L. Cates, Craig Blum, and Mark E. Swerdlik. Champaign, IL: Research Press (800-519-2707, www.researchpress.com)

BEHAVIOR FREQUENCY RECORDING LOG

Student: _____ Dates: _____

Behavior: _____

Observer: _____

Start/End Times	Activity	Monday	Tuesday	Wednesday	Thursday	Friday

Observer comments:

From *Effective RTI Training and Practice: Helping School and District Teams Improve Academic Performance and Social Behavior,* © 2011 Gary L. Cates, Craig Blum, and Mark E. Swerdlik. Champaign, IL: Research Press (800-519-2707, www.researchpress.com)

BEHAVIOR DESCRIPTION RECORDING LOG

Student: _____ Date: _____ Grade: _____

Teacher: _____ Observer: _____ Setting: _____

Directions: Please be as specific as possible.

Date	Time	Setting (where did the behavior take place?)	Task (what should student be doing?)	Behavior (what did student do?)	Consequence (how did you and/or other students react?)	Effect (what happened after these reactions?)

Comments:

From *Effective RTI Training and Practice: Helping School and District Teams Improve Academic Performance and Social Behavior,* © 2011 Gary L. Cates, Craig Blum, and Mark E. Swerdlik. Champaign, IL: Research Press (800-519-2707, www.researchpress.com)

BEHAVIOR OBSERVATION RECORDING FORM

Target Student Name: _____ Birth date: _____

School: _____ Teacher: _____

Observer: _____ Date: _____

	Behavior(s)	Definitions
1		
2		
3		
4		
5		

TARGET CHILD (TC)

	Behavior	1	2	3	4	5	6	7	8	9	10	11	12	13	14	15	16	17	18	19	20
1																					
2																					
3																					
4																					
5																					

	Behavior	21	22	23	24	25	26	27	28	29	30	31	32	33	34	35	36	37	38	39	40
1																					
2																					
3																					
4																					
5																					

COMPOSITE CHILD (CC)

	Behavior	1	2	3	4	5	6	7	8	9	10	11	12	13	14	15	16	17	18	19	20
1																					
2																					
3																					
4																					
5																					

	Behavior	21	22	23	24	25	26	27	28	29	30	31	32	33	34	35	36	37	38	39	40
1																					
2																					
3																					
4																					
5																					

TCB1 _____ TCB2 _____ TCB3 _____ TCB4 _____ TCB5 _____

CCB1 _____ CCB2 _____ CCB3 _____ CCB4 _____ CCB5 _____

To calculate percentages: (No. of Occurrences ÷ No. of Observations) × 100 = %.
For example, if there were 4 occurrences in 40 observations, (4 ÷ 40) × 100 = 10%

DAILY BEHAVIOR REPORT CARD

Date: _____ Teacher: _____ Student: _____

0 = No   1 = Yes

	Be Safe	Be Respectful	Be Ready		Teacher Initials
	Keep hands, feet, and objects to self	Use kind words and actions	Follow directions	Have needed materials	
Reading	0 1	0 1	0 1	0 1	
Recess	0 1	0 1	0 1	0 1	
Math	0 1	0 1	0 1	0 1	
Lunch	0 1	0 1	0 1	0 1	
Social Studies	0 1	0 1	0 1	0 1	
Recess	0 1	0 1	0 1	0 1	
Language Arts	0 1	0 1	0 1	0 1	
Science	0 1	0 1	0 1	0 1	

Total Points = _____   Today _____ %   Goal _____ %

Points possible = 32

Parent/guardian signature _____

From *Effective RTI Training and Practice: Helping School and District Teams Improve Academic Performance and Social Behavior,* © 2011 Gary L. Cates, Craig Blum, and Mark E. Swerdlik. Champaign, IL: Research Press (800-519-2707, www.researchpress.com)

TREATMENT INTEGRITY FORM

Implementer: _____   Intervention: _____

Observer: _____   School: _____

Student: _____   Time/Location: _____

Grade: _____   Teacher: _____

Step	Date	Date	Date	Date	Date
1.					
2.					
3.					
4.					
5.					
Daily Integrity Percentage	_____ %	_____ %	_____ %	_____ %	_____ %

About the Authors

GARY L. CATES earned his PhD from Mississippi State University and is an associate professor of psychology at Illinois State University. He teaches and conducts clinical supervision of graduate students related to assessment and intervention of academic and social behavior problems. He also coordinates the Academic Intervention and Consultation Service at the Psychological Services Center at ISU. Dr. Cates has authored or co-authored numerous research studies and national presentations. His primary research interests include the prevention and remediation of academic skills deficits, differential effectiveness and efficiency of academic interventions and learning strategies, and applied behavior analysis in educational settings. Dr. Cates is certified as a school psychologist in Illinois and also holds national certification in school psychology. His current consultation work primarily focuses on the implementation and evaluation of Response to Intervention models, with strong emphasis on data-based decision making. He currently is working with numerous schools in training staff to implement and sustain Response to Intervention procedures.

CRAIG BLUM is an assistant professor at Illinois State University in the Special Education Department. His research interests and expertise are in Response to Intervention for social behavior, Positive Behavior Intervention and Supports (PBIS), functional assessment in schools, and use of technology to teach emergent literacy skills to children with or at risk for disability. Dr. Blum publishes peer-reviewed research and presents to general and special educators locally and nationally. He has worked as a consultant with school districts on how to collect data on social behavior and integrate them into an RTI model.

MARK E. SWERDLIK is a professor of psychology, Coordinator of the Graduate Programs in School Psychology, and a clinical supervisor in the Psychological Services Center at Illinois State University, where he has been involved as a university educator of school psychologists for more than 30 years. He is a former school psychologist and currently maintains an independent practice of school psychology as a licensed clinical psychologist. Dr. Swerdlik is a Fellow of the American Psychological Association–Division of School Psychology. He has been awarded a Diplomate in School Psychology from the American Board of Professional Psychology and a Diplomate in Assessment Psychology from the American Board of Assessment Psychology. He has worked as a trainer, consultant, and program evaluator for schoolwide reform efforts such as the Flexible Student Services Model since its first implementation in Illinois in 1998. Currently, he serves as a regional evaluator for the statewide implementation of RTI in Illinois. Dr. Swerdlik has provided training in all components of RTI for a number of school districts in the Midwest and has widely presented and published his work related to this RTI initiative.

INSTRUCTIONS FOR USE OF CD

The CD that accompanies this book contains PDF documents that may be printed out and reproduced for noncommercial use by the purchaser.

The CD also contains a Microsoft Excel® template and six Microsoft PowerPoint® presentations, both of which may be modified for noncommercial use by the purchaser.

To modify a PowerPoint or Excel file, open the CD and copy the desired file to your computer's hard drive. Next, open the copied PowerPoint or Excel file and make your changes. Be sure to save the changes before closing the modified file. (We recommend that you assign a new name to the file; use the Save As function under the File menu/tab.)

Notes

To open the PDF files, you must have Adobe Reader® installed on your computer. Adobe Reader, which is free, may be downloaded at http://get.adobe.com/reader/

To open the Excel files, you must have Microsoft Excel installed on your computer.

To open the PowerPoint files, you must have Microsoft PowerPoint installed on your computer.